From Your Friends at **The MAILBOX®**

COMPREHENSION CONNECTIONS

Build Comprehension Skills With Science & Social Studies Passages

Grade 2

Project Editor
Amy Erickson

Writers
Rebecca Brudwick, Lisa Buchholz,
Vicki Dabrowka, Erin Harp

Editors
Deborah T. Kalwat, Leanne Stratton

Art Coordinator
Donna K. Teal

Artists
Teresa R. Davidson, Theresa Lewis Goode, Nick Greenwood,
Sheila Krill, Mary Lester, Kimberly Richard,
Rebecca Saunders, Donna K. Teal

Cover Artists
Nick Greenwood, Clevell Harris, Kimberly Richard

www.themailbox.com

©2001 by THE EDUCATION CENTER, INC.
All rights reserved.
ISBN #1-56234-426-9

Except as provided for herein, no part of this publication may be reproduced or transmitted in any form or by any means, electronic or mechanical, including photocopying, recording, or storing in any information storage and retrieval system or electronic online bulletin board, without prior written permission from The Education Center, Inc. Permission is given to the original purchaser to reproduce patterns and reproducibles for individual classroom use only and not for resale or distribution. Reproduction for an entire school or school system is prohibited. Please direct written inquiries to The Education Center, Inc., P.O. Box 9753, Greensboro, NC 27429-0753. The Education Center®, *The Mailbox*®, and the mailbox/post/grass logo are registered trademarks of The Education Center, Inc. All other brand or product names are trademarks or registered trademarks of their respective companies.

Manufactured in the United States
10 9 8 7 6 5 4 3 2

TABLE OF CONTENTS

Making Connections 3
   Strategies for before, during, & after reading
About This Book 5
Living Things
   Factors that influence growth 6
   Animal groups 7
   Animal habitats 8
Plants
   Parts of a flowering plant 9
   Life cycles 10
   Plant groups 11
Mammals
   Adaptations 12
   Camouflage 13
   Observing 14
Insects
   Interdependence of insects & plants 15
   Incomplete metamorphosis of a dragonfly 16
   Friends & enemies 17
Reptiles/Amphibians
   Extinction of dinosaurs 18
   Caring for young 19
   Frog's life cycle 20
Weather
   Observations 21
   Folklore 22
   Influence on daily life 23
Solar System
   Constellations 24
   Planets 25
   Earth's rotation 26
Matter
   States 27
   Changes to states of matter 28
   Sink & float 29
Forces & Energy
   Magnets 30
   Kinds of motion 31
   Gravity 32
Culture
   Native Americans 33
   The New Year 34
   Folktales 35

Then & Now
   Homes 36
   River travel 37
   Bread making 38
Geography
   Rural, suburban, & urban communities 39
   Man-made changes to the earth 40
   Maps 41
Economics
   Producers & consumers 42
   Milk from cow to table 43
   Division of labor 44
Civics & Government
   Laws 45
   Citizenship 46
   U.S. Constitution 47
The United States
   General information 48
   Capital 49
   Mount Rushmore 50
Historical Figures
   George Washington 51
   Ben Franklin 52
   Helen Keller 53
Inventions
   Radio 54
   Printing press 55
   Sewing machine 56
Famous Firsts
   Amelia Earhart 57
   Discovery of the North Pole 58
   Wilma Rudolph 59
Graphic Organizers 60
Answer Keys 62

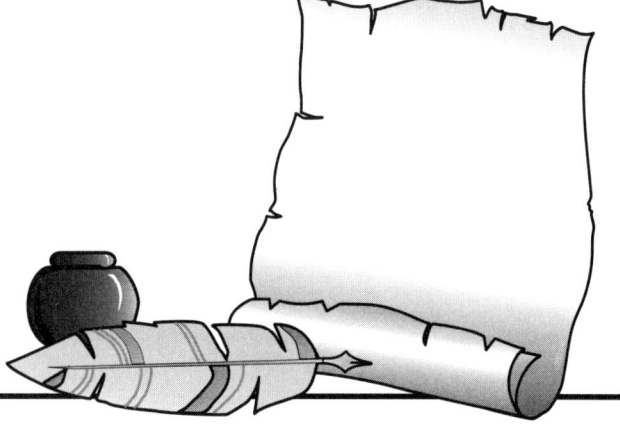

MAKING CONNECTIONS

What's the key to comprehension? Connections! Connections between words and meanings, between text and concepts, and between text and prior knowledge. Not only do these connections help students understand what they read, but they help them recall it, too!

Most students do not make these connections on their own, though. They need to be taught how. Learning a variety of strategies that they can use before, during, or after reading helps youngsters make these links and boosts comprehension.

> **Choose from among the tried-and-true strategies described here to match your students' needs. They're perfect for promoting comprehension of the passages in this book and of countless other reading materials!**

Before Reading

What do students already know about a topic? What misconceptions do they have? What experiences have they had with the concepts? The answers to these questions all relate to prior knowledge—the information and experiences that a student brings to a reading situation.

> Prior knowledge has a tremendous impact on comprehension because readers combine information from text with what they already know in order to gain meaning. Tap into prior knowledge and increase comprehension with the quick and easy ideas below.

- **It's in the Cards!:** Invite students to brainstorm words related to the reading topic. Write each word on a separate card. Ask students to group the cards and to explain their reasoning. If desired, post the grouped cards on a board. After youngsters read the text, have them revisit the groupings and make changes as appropriate to reflect the information they learned.

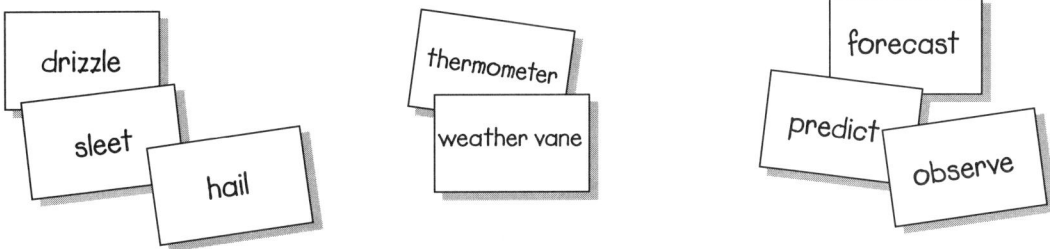

- **Set a Purpose:** Guide each youngster in setting a purpose for reading, such as finding the answer to a question or finding the most important sentence in a passage.

- **Take a Look!:** Encourage students to read the title and look at the illustrations. Then have them share their observations and predict what they will learn from the text.

During Reading

Does it make sense? This all-important question is one that good readers frequently ask themselves. In fact, they constantly self-monitor their reading. Use the following ideas to heighten students' awareness of their comprehension as they read.

- **Think-Alouds:** Model this strategy by sharing your thought processes as you read aloud, interrupting your reading to verbally insert your predictions, context clues that you use, things you're wondering about…in short, any thoughts you have about the text. As you resume your reading, model how you pick up the train of thought where you left off. After several demonstrations, have students try the strategy in small groups.

- **Partner Up!:** This idea works well for multiparagraph passages. Pair students. One student in each pair reads the first paragraph to his partner. The listener summarizes the paragraph. The partners switch roles and then continue reading and summarizing the rest of the passage.

- **Stop and Restate:** Encourage each student to read a passage in small sections, stopping after each section to silently restate what he has read. If he has trouble restating at any point, he rereads the relevant section.

After Reading

So what was the passage about? Do you agree with the author? Continue the reading process with questions like these to help students fully understand the text. Here are some other effective follow-ups:

- **Picture-Perfect:** As soon as students finish reading a passage, invite them to describe any pictures they made in their heads as they were reading.

- **In Search Of:** Ask students literal and inferential questions about the passage. Have them determine whether each answer is "right there" in the passage, whether they need to "read between the lines" to find it, or whether they need to use their own opinions and experiences to answer.

- **Graphic Organizers:** Have youngsters organize and process the information they learned from reading by having each one use a copy of a provided graphic organizer (see pages 60 and 61) or inviting them to make their own webs and charts. For a whole-class follow-up, make a transparency of a graphic organizer and complete it with students.

ABOUT THIS BOOK

Overview

It's no secret that time is a precious commodity for teachers. So why not maximize it (and student learning!) by reinforcing reading skills and content area concepts at the same time? This book will help you do exactly that. Each comprehension unit is based on common science or social studies standards. Because each unit is three pages long, students have multiple opportunities to read about the same topic or theme. This repeated exposure helps them build prior knowledge and further strengthens comprehension.

Most text lends itself to practice with a few different comprehension skills. The passages in this book are no exception. The most significant skills on each page are indicated at the top of it.

Before Students Start

The words below are used in student directions in this book. For best results, familiarize students with the words before assigning any pages that include them.

- *Passage:* Explain that a passage is a piece of writing—not a story.
- *Thoughts* and *Ideas:* Many of the questions in this book ask students to write their thoughts or ideas. Point out that there is no one right answer for any of these questions, but that students should be able to support their reasoning.
- *Column:* Tell students that one way to organize words is by placing them in labeled columns, grouped under the appropriate headings.

In Every Unit

- **Prior Knowledge Question:** A question above each passage helps you set the stage for students' reading.

- **Words to Know:** Critical vocabulary words are noted. To introduce a word, try one or more of these ideas:
  — Discuss any multiple meanings.
  — Help students use familiar word parts to determine the word and its meaning.
  — Demonstrate what the word means; show the item it names or a picture of it.
  — Have students predict the meaning and an appropriate use of the word by dictating a sentence for it. Ask them to read the passage to check their ideas and then revise the sentence if needed.

- **Passage:** Encourage students to read each passage more than once to increase fluency and, as a result, comprehension. Some students may benefit from using line markers to keep their place as they read.

- **Brain Builder:** A question for each passage promotes reflection and higher-level thinking. Use it as part of the assignment rather than as a bonus in order to ensure that all students have rich, thought-provoking experiences with the text.

Name _____   Context clues, details, drawing conclusions

What are some things that help you grow?

Key Ingredients

When you bake a cake, you need to use the right ingredients. You also need to use them in the right amounts. If you do not, the cake will not come out the way it should. The same thing is true for living things. Plants and animals need certain things to grow. If they do not get them in the right amounts, they will not grow well.

Living things need air to breathe. They need water, too. If plants do not get enough water, they might wilt. If people do not get enough water, they will not stay healthy.

Living things need food to get energy. Plants use sunlight to make their own food. People get food from plants and animals.

Words to Know

ingredient   amount

energy

1. **Look** back at the title. **Circle** the letter for the answer below that tells what *key* means.

   a. recipe   b. a tool for locks   c. important

2. **Read** the words below. **Circle** three things that all living things need.

   air   sleep   soil   water   milk   food

3. **Look** back in the passage. **Underline** the sentence that tells where people get energy.

4. What might happen if a plant does not get enough sunlight? Why?

   _____
   _____

On the back of this sheet, draw a flower that has everything it needs to grow. Then draw a flower that does not. Write a sentence for each picture.

Brain Builder

©2001 The Education Center, Inc. • Comprehension Connections • TEC4110 • Key p. 62

LIVING THINGS: *Factors that influence growth*

Name _____

Comparison and contrast, reading a chart

What are some ways that animals are different?

Words to Know
scales   moist
     gills

Animals, Animals Everywhere!

Do you know that there are more than a million kinds of animals? They come in all shapes and sizes. Some have fur, hair, or feathers. Others might have scales or moist skin.
Many animals live on land. They breathe through lungs. They might walk, hop, or crawl. Some animals live in water and breathe through gills. Most of them use tail fins to swim. Some animals live on land part of the time and in water the rest of the time. Other animals spend a lot of time in the air. There are all kinds of animals everyplace you look!

Look at the chart below. **Answer** the questions.

Animal	What covers its body?	Where does it live?
cat	fur	on land
angelfish	scales	in water
frog	moist skin	in and near water
robin	feathers	in the air and in nests

1. **Think** about where fish live. How do they breathe? _____

2. One animal shown on the chart uses gills to breathe when it is young. It uses lungs when it is older. What animal is it? _____

3. **Write** how you decided on your answer for question number 2. _____

Brain Builder

Think about the passage and the chart. On the back of this sheet, write one way that cats and robins are alike. Write one way they are different.

©2001 The Education Center, Inc. • *Comprehension Connections* • TEC4110 • Key p. 62

LIVING THINGS: *Animal groups*

Name _____   Context clues, details, main idea

What things does every animal need for a home?

Words to Know
koala
shelter
prairie dog

Home, Sweet Habitat

There's no place like home! Different animals need different types of homes. Every animal lives in a habitat that has the things it needs.

One thing an animal needs is food. A house mouse can eat many kinds of food. This makes it easy for it to find a place it can live. Wild koalas do not eat as many foods. They eat only the leaves of a kind of tree that grows in Australia. That is the only country where they can live.

Animals need shelter, too. Trees make good shelters for many animals. There are not a lot of trees where prairie dogs live, though. They dig their homes underground. Their burrows help keep them safe.

1. **Look** back in the passage. **Circle** the word that means "animal home."

2. **Complete** each sentence with a word below. *(Hint: You will not use one of the words.)*

   | burrows | safe | tree | country |

   a. Australia is a _____.
   b. Some animals live in underground homes called _____.
   c. A shelter helps keep an animal _____.

3. What is the passage mostly about? **Circle** the letter for the best answer.

   a. Prairie dogs live in burrows.
   b. Every animal eats food.
   c. Animals live in homes that are right for them.
   d. Trees make good homes for birds.

Think about the passage. What are two ways that people's homes are like animals' homes? Write your ideas on the back of this sheet.

Brain Builder

LIVING THINGS: *Animal habitats*

Name _____   Details, drawing conclusions, main idea

What are the parts of a flower?

Words to Know
minerals
travel
fruit

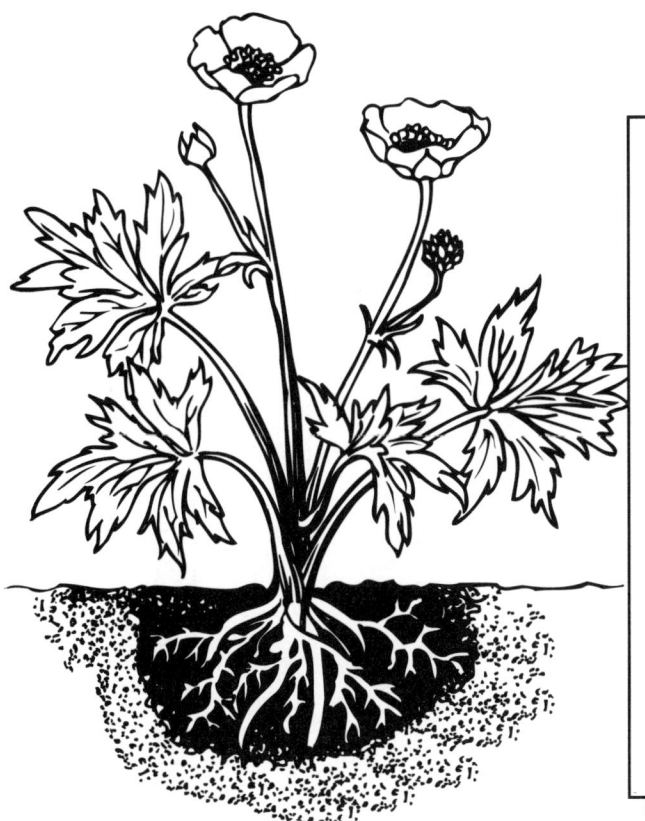

From far away, a flower garden looks like a sea of color! If you look more closely, you will see that the flowers are made of many parts. Every flower has roots that hold it in the ground. The roots take in water and minerals from the soil. Every flower has a stem that holds it up. The stem is like a road for the plant. The water and minerals travel from the roots, up the stem, and to other parts of the plant. The leaves on a flower help feed it. They use sunlight to make food. Every flower makes fruit. The fruit has seeds that help make new, colorful flowers.

1. **Draw** a line from each flower part to the words that tell about it.
   - a. stem •   • makes new flowers
   - b. leaf •   • helps feed the flower
   - c. fruit •   • holds up the flower
   - d. seed •   • holds seeds

2. The roots of a flower have two jobs. What are they? _____
   _____
   _____

3. What is a good title for this passage? Why? _____
   _____
   _____

Brain Builder

Why do you think the author says that a flower stem is like a road? Write your ideas on the back of this sheet.

©2001 The Education Center, Inc. • *Comprehension Connections* • TEC4110 • Key p. 62

PLANTS: *Parts of a flowering plant*

Name _____

Contrast, details, sequencing

What is a cycle?

Words to Know

seed   fern   ripe

How Does Your Garden Grow?

Think about a circle. A circle does not have a beginning or an end. A plant life cycle is like a circle. It tells how a plant grows and makes new plants. A seed is important in a flower's life cycle. The seed grows into a small plant called a seedling. If the seedling gets the right care, it grows into an adult plant. The plant grows a flower. The flower makes seeds, and the cycle continues.

Not all plants have seeds, though. Ferns have spores instead. Spores look like tiny brown spots. They grow on the underside of leaves. When the spores are ripe, they fall off the leaves and might grow into new plants.

1. **Number** the sentences below to show a flower's life cycle. *(The first one has been marked for you.)*

   ___ A flower grows on the plant.
   _1_ A seed turns into a seedling.
   ___ The flower makes seeds.
   ___ The seedling grows into a plant.

2. **Look** back in the passage. **Underline** the sentence that tells how spores look.

3. How is the life cycle of a rose different from the life cycle of a fern? _____

On the back of this sheet, draw and label four pictures that show the life cycle of a flower. Draw an arrow from one picture to the next.

PLANTS: *Life cycles*

Name _____   *Comparison, details*

How is a rose different from a pine tree?

Words to Know
blossoms
cones
deciduous

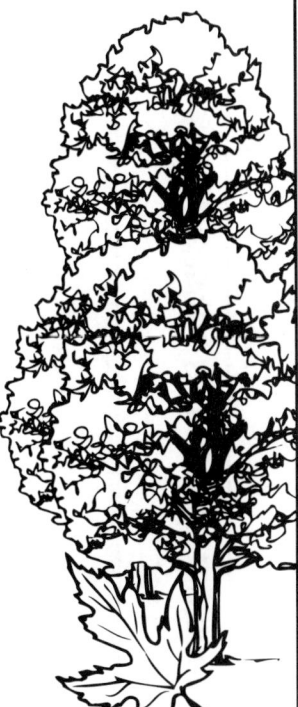

Speaking of Plants

There are many ways to describe plants. You might tell how they look or smell. You might tell how big they are. Another way is to tell what kinds of plants they are.

<u>Flowering plants</u> have blossoms. The blossoms make fruits with seeds. Roses, apple trees, and beans are all flowering plants.

<u>Evergreen</u> trees do not have blossoms, fruit, or leaves. They have cones with seeds. They have pine needles, too. The needles stay on the trees all year. Pine and fir trees are evergreens.

Oak and other kinds of trees with leaves are called <u>deciduous</u>. The leaves change color in the fall. Then they fall off the tree.

Now you know more ways to describe the plants you see!

1. **Think** about the underlined words in the passage.
   Read the sentences below.
   Circle yes or no.

   a. Pine trees have leaves.   yes   no
   b. Apple trees can make blossoms.   yes   no
   c. The leaves on an oak tree change color in the spring.   yes   no
   d. Fir trees have cones and needles.   yes   no
   e. Roses make seeds.   yes   no

2. How is a fruit like a pinecone? _____

   _____

Brain Builder

Think about the passage. On the back of this sheet, explain how to tell a pine tree from an oak tree.

©2001 The Education Center, Inc. • Comprehension Connections • TEC4110 • Key p. 62

PLANTS: *Plant groups* 11

Name _____

Context clues, details, main idea

What are some things that help mammals survive?

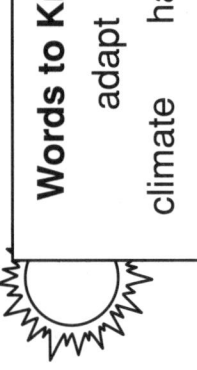

Words to Know
adapt
climate   habitat

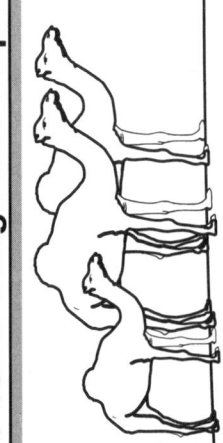

Right at Home!

Some mammals live where it is cold. Some live where it is warm. Others live where the climate does not stay the same. Mammals need to adapt to their habitats to survive. Sometimes it takes many years for them to change.

Whales have adapted to cold habitats. They have a lot of fat under their skin. The blubber helps whales stay warm.

Camels have adapted to hot, dry habitats. They <u>store</u> fat in their humps. Their bodies use the fat to make water.

Foxes live where the climate changes. In the winter, foxes grow thicker fur on their tails. The thick fur helps keep them warm.

When mammals adapt to their habitats, they make themselves right at home!

1. **Look** back in the passage. **Circle** the word that means almost the same as "adapt."

2. **Use** the words below to complete the sentences. *(Hint: You will not use one of the words.)*

   blubber   survive   thinner   adapt

   a. Mammals adapt to help them _____.
   b. _____ helps keep whales warm.
   c. In the summer, foxes have _____ fur.

3. **Look** at the underlined word in the passage. **Circle** the letter of the word below that tells what it means.

   a. shop   b. keep   c. buy

4. **Look** back in the passage. **Underline** the sentence that best tells the main idea.

Brain Builder

What might happen if a mammal does not adapt to its habitat? Why? Write your ideas on the back of this sheet.

MAMMALS: *Adaptations*

©2001 The Education Center, Inc. • *Comprehension Connections* • TEC4110 • Key p. 62

Name _____

Context clues, drawing conclusions, main idea

Why is it important for some mammals to hide in their environments?

Words to Know
camouflage
blend   hare

Hide-and-Seek

A lot of mammals try to hide from their enemies. Some mammals hide behind rocks or trees. Other mammals hide right out in the open! Camouflage makes them hard to see. Camouflage is a color, pattern, or shape. It helps a mammal blend into the environment.

Some mice have fur that is the same color as the rocks, wood, and sand where they live. The mice fool their enemies because they can hide in plain sight. They protect themselves with camouflage.

Some mammals can change color. A snowshoe hare is white like snow in winter. It turns brown like dirt and rocks in the summer. Camouflage helps mammals stay safe all year long!

1. **Underline** the sentences in the passage that tell what *camouflage* means.
2. **Circle** the word in the passage that means "keep safe."
3. Why is camouflage important to some mammals?
   _____
   _____
4. Why do you think the author chose the title "Hide-and-Seek"?
   _____
   _____

Think about the passage. On the back of this sheet, draw and label a picture of a snowshoe hare in the summer. Then draw and label a picture of it in the winter.

Name _____   Context clues, details, inferences

What can you learn about a chimpanzee by watching it?

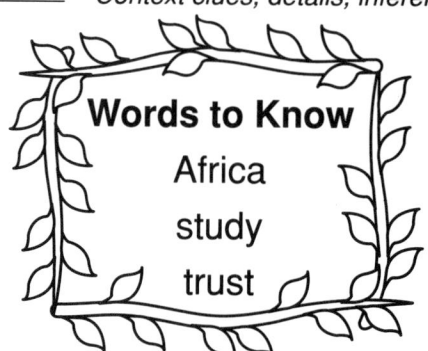

Words to Know
Africa
study
trust

Learn by Watching

What is one way to learn about a mammal? By watching it in its home! That is what Jane Goodall did. She went to Africa to study chimpanzees. At first, the chimps were scared of Jane. They did not want her to get close. After a long time, the chimps began to trust her.

Jane learned a lot about the chimps by observing them. Jane found out something that surprised many people. She found out that chimps are a lot like people. Jane saw chimps do many things that people do. She saw them hunt for meat. She saw them use sticks for tools. She saw them solve problems. She found out that chimps even have feelings!

1. **Look** back in the passage. **Circle** the word that means "watching."

2. **Think** about the passage. **List** three ways that chimps are like people.
   _____
   _____

3. Why do you think the chimps began to trust Jane?
   _____
   _____

4. **Read** the words below. **Circle** the three words that best tell about Jane Goodall.
   watchful   rushed   brave   scientist

Think about the passage. On the back of this sheet, tell about Jane Goodall in your own words.

Brain Builder

Name _____   *Context clues, details, drawing conclusions*

In what ways do plants and insects help each other?

Words to Know
nectar   pollen
depend

Insect and Plant Pals

What do you see when you look in a garden? You might see pretty flowers or yummy fruits. You might see a lot of insects, too. Insects and plants depend on each other. Some insects feed on the nectar from flowers. Other insects eat plant stems, leaves, or fruit. Some insects lay their eggs on plants.

Plants need insects, too. Bees and butterflies carry pollen from plant to plant as they gather nectar. Plants need the pollen to make flowers and seeds. The next time you're in a garden, think about the ways plants and insects help each other!

1. **Look** back in the passage. **Underline** two kinds of insects that carry pollen to help plants grow.

2. One reason plants need insects is _____.

3. One reason insects need plants is _____.

4. **Circle** the word below that means almost the same as "need."

    want   feed   depend

Think about the passage. What might happen if there were no more insects? Write your ideas on the back of this sheet.

©2001 The Education Center, Inc. • Comprehension Connections • TEC4110 • Key p. 62

Name _____   *Inferences, main idea, sequencing*

Where do dragonflies live?

Words to Know
nymph   shed   dart

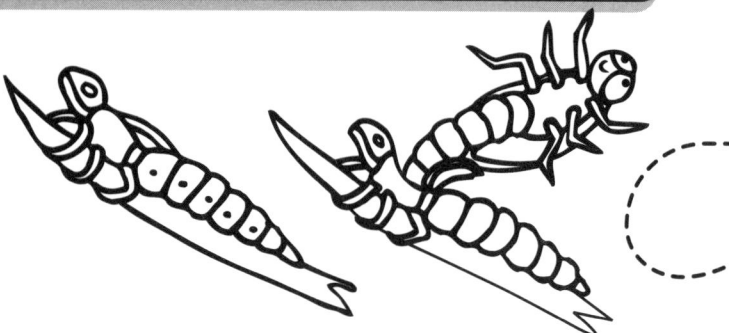

The Changing Dragonfly

Insects might be good jumpers, diggers, or swimmers. A dragonfly is one of the best flyers. It can fly backward and forward. Some dragonflies can even fly faster than birds! A young dragonfly cannot fly at all, though.

A young dragonfly is called a nymph. A nymph does not have wings. It lives and grows in the water. When it is ready, the nymph crawls out of the water onto a plant. Then it sheds its old skin. It becomes an adult dragonfly with wings. When its wings and body are stronger, the dragonfly darts away. What a change from an insect that once lived in water and had no wings!

1. **What** is a young dragonfly called? _____

2. **Think** about a dragonfly's life. **Number** the sentences below in the correct order.
   ____ When the insect is stronger, it flies.
   ____ The nymph sheds its skin.
   ____ A dragonfly nymph climbs onto a plant.
   ____ The insect has wings, but it is weak.

3. Where do dragonfly nymphs live? _____

4. What can a dragonfly do as an adult that it could not do as a nymph?
   _____

On the back of this sheet, draw four pictures to show the parts of a dragonfly's life. Make them look like a comic strip.

Brain Builder

16 **INSECTS:** *Incomplete metamorphosis of a dragonfly*

Name _____   *Completing a chart, context clues, details*

How do insects help people?

Words to Know
mosquito aphid
pollinate

Insect Friends and Enemies

Some insect pests can cause a lot of trouble! Bees sometimes sting people. Mosquitoes bite and sometimes make people sick. Aphids eat garden plants. Some grasshoppers can even wipe out a farmer's whole crop!

Not all insects are pests, though. Some insects help people. Ladybugs help them by eating aphids. Praying mantises and wasps do, too. Bees and butterflies pollinate plants. Then the plants can make seeds for new plants. Farmers love these insects. There are all kinds of insects in the world. Some are pests, but many of them are our friends!

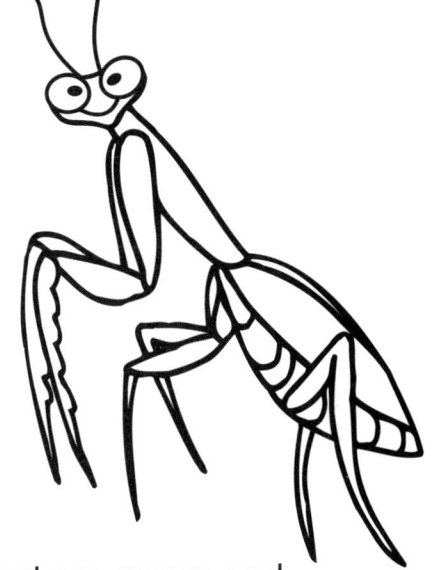

1. **Circle** the word in the passage that means "plants that are grown and gathered."

2. **List** two ways insects can help people.

   a. _____

   b. _____

3. **Draw** an **X** for each insect below to show whether it is a friend or a pest to farmers. *(Hint: One insect is both.)*

	friend	enemy
aphid		
ladybug		
praying mantis		
bee		

Brain Builder

Look back in the passage. Choose a kind of insect that helps people. On the back of this sheet, make a Help Wanted poster asking the insect to help you in your garden.

Name _____   Context clues, drawing conclusions, fact/opinion

Why do you think there are not any dinosaurs on earth?

Words to Know
blocked   reptile   asteroid

Dinosaur Doom

What happened to the dinosaurs? No one knows for sure. There are two main ideas about how these <u>reptiles</u> became extinct.

Some people think the <u>climate</u> on the earth changed. They think winters got very cold and summers got very hot. Dinosaurs could not have lived in this climate.

Other people think that a huge <u>asteroid</u> crashed into the earth. The asteroid would have made large clouds of dust. The dust would have blocked the sun's light from the earth. It would have been very cold. Plants would have died. The dinosaurs would have been too cold and hungry to live.

1. **Look** back in the passage. **Circle** the word that means "no longer living."

2. **Look** at the underlined words in the passage. **Use** each one to complete a sentence below.

   a. If an _____ hit the earth, it would have made big dust clouds.

   b. Dinosaurs were _____.

   c. _____ means "weather over a long time."

3. **Read** each sentence. **Write** "fact" or "opinion."

   a. Dinosaurs are extinct. _____

   b. An asteroid made dust clouds that cooled the earth. _____

   c. Dinosaurs walked the earth long ago. _____

Brain Builder

Why do you think no one knows what happened to the dinosaurs? Write your ideas on the back of this sheet.

©2001 The Education Center, Inc. • Comprehension Connections • TEC4110 • Key p. 62

REPTILES/AMPHIBIANS: *Extinction of dinosaurs*

Name _____ Context clues, details, inferences

What do you know about amphibian and reptile parents?

Mamas and Papas

Reptiles and most amphibians come from eggs. Many of their parents lay the eggs and leave them. Other amphibians and reptiles stay close to the eggs. One reptile that takes good care of its eggs is the Indian python. She wraps her body around the eggs. She shakes to keep them warm until they hatch.

One amphibian that takes good care of its eggs is the Darwin's frog. The male Darwin's frog watches over its eggs until they hatch into tadpoles. He swallows the tadpoles into a throat pouch. When they grow into froglets, he spits out the baby frogs. Some parents have very special ways of taking care of their babies!

Words to Know
amphibian
reptile
pouch

1. **Read** each sentence. **Circle** yes or no.

    a. All reptiles leave their eggs alone to hatch.   yes   no
    b. The female Indian python swallows her eggs.   yes   no
    c. The male Darwin's frog takes care of its babies.   yes   no
    d. Froglets are small frogs.   yes   no

2. **Read** the words below. **Write** each word in the correct column. *(Hint: One word will be used twice.)*

    | swallows   wraps   shakes   hatches   tadpoles |

    Darwin's frog   Indian python
    _____   _____
    _____   _____
    _____   _____

Brain Builder

How is the way an Indian python cares for its eggs different from the way that a Darwin's frog does? Write your ideas on the back of this sheet.

©2001 The Education Center, Inc. • *Comprehension Connections* • TEC4110 • Key p. 62

Name _____   Comparison and contrast, details

What do you know about the growth of frogs?

Words to Know
gills
breathe
metamorphosis

From Egg to Frog

A frog's body changes as it grows. The changes are called metamorphosis.

1. First, a frog lays its eggs in water. The eggs do not have shells. The eggs have a covering that is like jelly. It protects them.

2. Next, the frog eggs hatch into tadpoles. Tadpoles do not have legs. A tadpole has a tail. It breathes through gills like a fish.

3. A tadpole grows back legs and then front legs. The tadpole's lungs form so it can breathe air.

4. At last the tadpole's gills get smaller and disappear. Its tail gets smaller and disappears, too. The tadpole has grown into a froglet that can go on land!

---

1. **Look** back in the beginning of the passage. **Underline** the word that means "change."

2. **Read** each sentence below. **Circle** yes or no.

   a. Adult frogs breathe with gills.   yes   no
   b. Frog eggs have thin shells.   yes   no
   c. Tadpoles live in water.   yes   no

3. **Write** one way that a tadpole is different from a frog. _____
   _____

Frogs and people change as they grow. How are the changes alike? How are they different? Write your ideas on the back of this sheet.

Brain Builder

Name _____ Details, inference, main idea

How do forecasters study the weather?

Words to Know
predict
air pressure
container

Weather Watchers

"Today will be cloudy with a chance of rain. It will be a steamy 88 degrees." You might hear predictions like these from weather forecasters. They watch the weather and use tools to predict it.

One tool forecasters use is a thermometer. They use it to check the temperature. They have a tool to check air pressure, too. Air pressure tells whether a storm is on its way. Forecasters use a special container to measure rainfall. A weather vane tells us from which direction the wind is blowing. Forecasters also check wind speed. Watch the weather and make some predictions of your own!

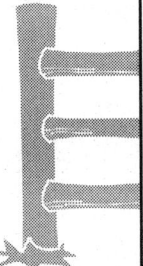

1. **Look** back in the passage.
   a. What tool tells wind direction? _____
   b. What tool tells whether the day is cold enough for it to snow?
   _____

2. What is the passage mostly about?
   _____

3. Weather forecasters help people do all of the following things except one. **Circle** the correct letter to show what they do not usually help people do.

   a. decide whether they need umbrellas
   b. choose the right clothes for the weather
   c. know where to buy umbrellas
   d. know whether it will be a good day to fly kites

Brain Builder

Why do you think it is important to measure the weather? Write your ideas on the back of this sheet.

Name _____   Context clues, details, drawing conclusions

What are some ways that people can tell what the weather will be?

Words to Know
nature
shadow
hints

Nature's Weather Hints

A closed pinecone means rain, right? That is what some people think! Some people watch nature for hints about the weather. They use the hints to make weather predictions.

Some people think that a flower called morning glory can help tell the weather. They say that if its petals are open, it will be a nice day. Some people think cows can help, too. They say that if the cows are lying down, it will rain soon. Many people watch a groundhog on February 2 to learn about the weather. They think that there will be six more weeks of winter if he sees his shadow. Look out a window. There may be more weather hints outside!

1. **Look** back in the passage. What weather hint do some people say cows give?
   _____

2. What word in the passage means "clues"? _____

3. **Think** about the passage. **Complete** each sentence to tell what some people believe about the weather.

   a. A groundhog sees his shadow. There will be _____
   _____.

   b. Pinecones are closed. There will be _____.

   c. Morning glory flower petals are open. It will be _____.

Are nature hints the best things to use to predict weather? Why or why not? Write your answer on the back of this sheet.

Brain Builder

©2001 The Education Center, Inc. • Comprehension Connections • TEC4110 • Key p. 62

22 WEATHER: *Folklore*

Drawing conclusions, reading a chart

Name _____

What things helped you decide what to wear today?

Words to Know

plan   travel   forecast

Every Day Is Different!

The weather can change from day to day. Sometimes it is hard to know what it will be. Weather forecasts help us plan what to wear. If the forecast is for cold weather, we might want to wear jackets. If it is for warm weather, we might wear shorts. If the forecast says it will be cloudy, it is smart to take an umbrella. If it says there will be snow, ice, or fog, we need to be careful. Traveling might not be safe.

Look at the forecast and key below. **Answer** the questions.

1. **Think** about the passage. What might be good to wear on Monday? Why?
   _____

2. On what days should you plan to take an umbrella? Why?
   _____

3. **Look** at the forecast. **Read** the words below. **Circle** the two things you might do during the week.

   build a snowman   fly a kite
   wear a raincoat   go sledding

Forecast Key

windy   snowy
rainy   sunny
cloudy stormy

Sunday	Monday	Tuesday	Wednesday	Thursday	Friday	Saturday
windy	sunny	sunny	windy	cloudy	rainy	stormy
warm	hot	warm	warm	cool	cool	cold

Brain Builder

Look at the chart. What do you notice about the temperature during the week? Write your ideas on the back of this sheet.

WEATHER: Influence on daily life

©2001 The Education Center, Inc. • *Comprehension Connections* • TEC4110 • Key p. 63

23

Name _____

Context clues, details, drawing conclusions

What do you see in the sky at night?

Pictures in the Stars

Look at the sky on a clear, dark night. What do you see? Do you see pictures of animals or people? Some people do! They see the pictures in groups of stars. The stars make only part of the pictures, though. People imagine that lines join them. It is like doing dot-to-dot puzzles from far away! Star pictures are called constellations.

There are 88 main constellations. Long ago, people made up stories about them. One story is about a hunter named Orion. He hunts animals in the stars. The star pictures of his two dogs are near him. Some other constellations are a lion, a bear, and a horse with wings. Star pictures light up the night sky with wonderful stories!

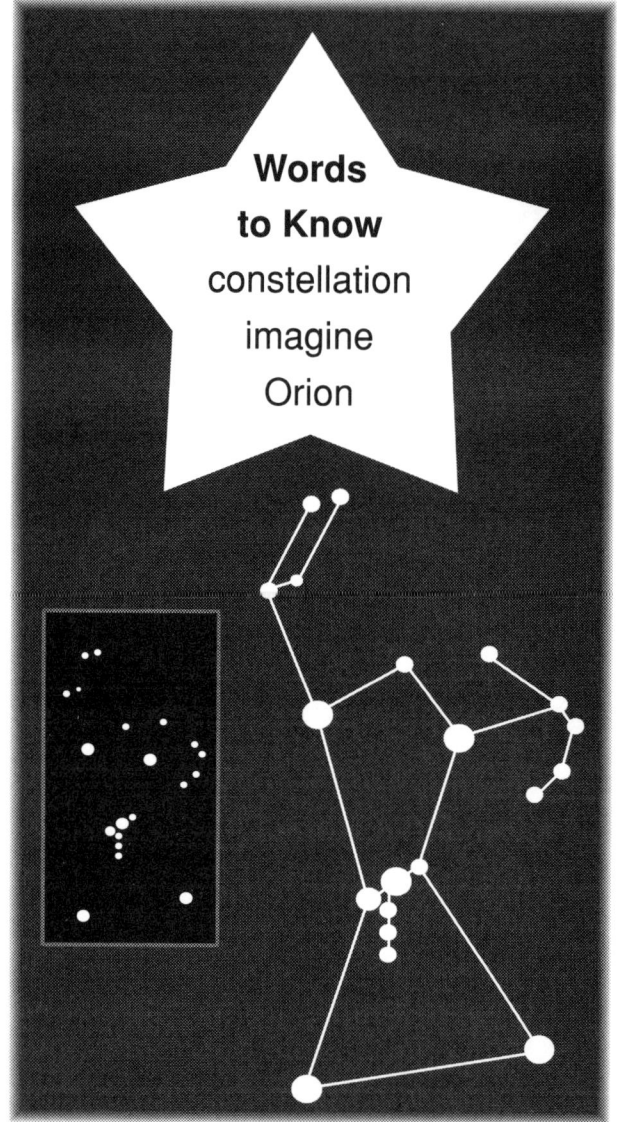

Words to Know
constellation
imagine
Orion

1. **Think** about the passage. **Complete** the sentences below.
   a. Groups of stars that make pictures are called _____.
   b. Many star picture stories are about _____ or people.

2. **Circle** the word below that tells about Orion.
   dragon   lion   hunter   horse

3. **Look** back in the passage. **Underline** the sentence that tells what animal constellations are near Orion.

Look at the pictures of Orion on this sheet. Why does the author say that stars make only part of a constellation? Write your ideas on the back of this sheet.

Brain Builder

Name _____   Classification, context clues, drawing conclusions

What do you know about the planets?

Words to Know
solar system
giant
gases

The Sun's Family

What spins all the time but never gets dizzy? A planet! Our solar system has nine planets that spin as they go around the sun.

Mercury, Venus, Earth, and Mars are the closest planets to the sun. They are called the rocky planets. Moons travel around Earth and Mars.

Jupiter, Saturn, Uranus, and Neptune are giant planets. They are made mostly of gases. <u>They are light for their size.</u> If you could put Saturn in water, it would float! Each of these planets has rings and moons.

We do not know much about Pluto. No spaceships have visited it. Pluto is far away and very small. It might be made of rocks and ice.

1. **Draw** a square around each rocky planet. **Circle** each gas planet.

   Neptune   Mars   Mercury   Uranus

   Jupiter   Saturn   Venus   Earth

2. **Look** back in the passage. What does *light* mean in the underlined sentence? **Circle** the letter below to show your answer.

   a. not heavy   b. a lamp   c. to land

3. Why would Saturn float if it could be put in water? _____

   _____

4. Underline the sentences in the passage that tell why we do not know much about Pluto.

Why do you think the author chose the title "The Sun's Family"? Write your ideas on the back of this sheet.

Name _____

Why do you think we have day and night?

Context clues, details, main idea

Words to Know
rotation   planet
orbit   rotate

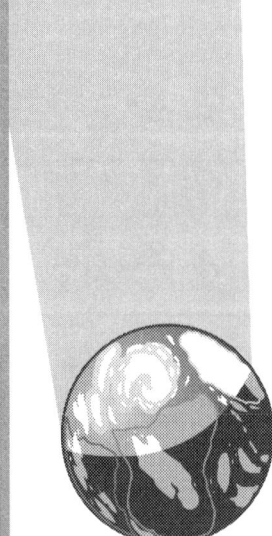

The sun is a huge ball of hot gas that gives off heat and light. Nine planets circle around the sun in paths called orbits. As the planets orbit, they spin like tops. This spinning is called rotation.

It takes Earth one day to make a full rotation. As Earth spins, it is daytime on the side that faces the sun. It is nighttime on the side that faces away from the sun. To people on Earth, it looks like the sun moves up and down. Don't be fooled, though! It is really Earth that is moving.

1. **Read** the words below. **Circle** the word that does not belong.

   spin   point   turn   rotate

2. **Look** back in the passage. What does *faces* mean in the underlined sentence? **Circle** the letter beside the correct answer below.
   a. the front part of the head
   b. sides
   c. looks toward

3. **Look** back in the passage. What are the two ways that planets move in space? _____

4. What is a good title for this passage? _____

Brain Builder: Why do you think it looks like the sun moves? Write your ideas on the back of this sheet.

SOLAR SYSTEM: *Earth's rotation*

©2001 The Education Center, Inc. • *Comprehension Connections* • TEC4110 • Key p. 63

Name _____   Context clues, details, inferences

What is matter?

Words to Know
helium
containers
invisible

Facts of the Matter

What is the same about apple juice, a car, and the air inside a balloon? They are all made of matter! Matter is anything that takes up space and has weight. Three kinds, or states, of matter are solids, liquids, and gases.

Balls, books, and crayons are solids. They have their own shapes. Water, milk, and soup are liquids. They are the same shapes as their containers. All liquids can be poured. Steam and helium are gases. They have no shape. They expand to fill their containers. Most gases are invisible.

Big, small, wet, or dry, matter is everywhere you look!

1. **Read** each sentence below. **Circle** true or false.

a. Most gases are colorful.	true	false
b. Juice has its own shape.	true	false
c. Many solids can be held.	true	false
d. All matter is heavy.	true	false

2. **Look** back in the passage. **Circle** the word that means "spread out."

3. Is chocolate milk a solid, liquid, or gas? _____

    How do you know? _____

    _____

Brain Builder

Think about the passage. On the back of this sheet, rewrite each false sentence in question number 1 to make it true.

Name _____

What happens when something melts?

Details, inferences

Words to Know
vapor spread
imagine

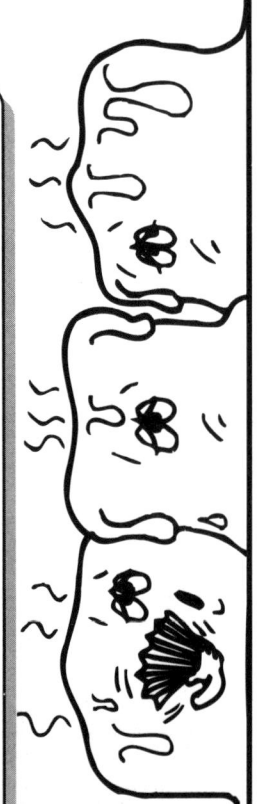

Water, Water Everywhere!

Water is a special kind of matter. It can be a solid, liquid, or gas. A freezer and a stove can help change water from one of these states to another.

The water in a glass is a liquid. It takes the shape of the glass. If the water spilled, it would spread out into a new shape. Imagine that the water is heated in a pan. Some of the water would turn into a gas called water vapor.

Now imagine that the water is poured into trays and put into the freezer. It would turn into ice cubes. Ice cubes have their own shape. When they start to get warm, though, they melt back into a liquid.

1. **Use** the words below to complete each sentence. (Hint: You will not use one of the words.)

vapor	change	liquid	heat

   a. Matter can _____ states.

   b. Water _____ is a gas.

   c. _____ and cold can change matter.

2. **Write** "solid," "liquid," or "gas."

   a. water in a bathtub _____

   b. ice on a skating rink _____

   c. vapor from a pan of hot soup _____

3. How can you change an ice cube into a liquid? _____

Brain Builder

Sometimes when a person eats ice cream, it changes from one state of matter to another. On the back of this sheet, explain how this might happen.

MATTER: Changes to states of matter

©2001 The Education Center, Inc. • *Comprehension Connections* • TEC4110 • Key p. 63

Name _____   Context clues, details, inferences

Why do some things float?

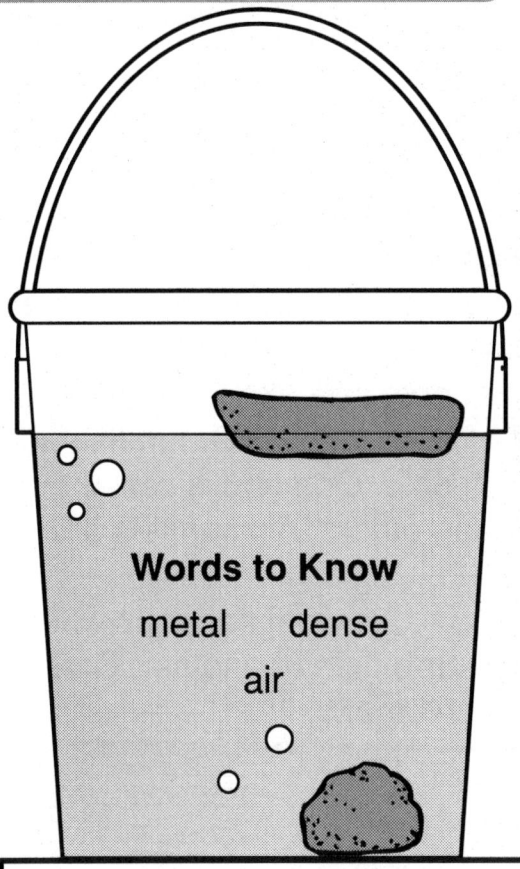

Words to Know
metal   dense
air

Water Wonders

What would happen if you dropped a ball of clay into a pail of water? It would sink to the bottom. Clay does not always sink in water, though. If the clay were shaped into a thin boat, it would float. It would float because it would hold a lot of air.

A nail, a car key, and many other metal things sink in water just as a clay ball does. They are very dense. A steel boat is different. It is big, heavy, and made of metal, but it floats on water. The air inside the boat makes the boat less dense.

<u>Sometimes it is hard to know if something will sink or float just by looking at it!</u>

1. **Look** back in the passage. What does *sink* mean in the underlined sentence? **Circle** the correct letter below to show your answer.

    a. a place to do dishes
    b. go in a hole
    c. go under water

2. What holds more air: a clay ball or a clay boat? _____

3. **Look** back in the passage. **Underline** the sentence that tells why a clay boat would float.

4. Why does a steel boat float? _____
_____

Brain Builder

Why does the author say that it is hard to know if something will float just by looking at it? Write your ideas on the back of this sheet.

©2001 The Education Center, Inc. • *Comprehension Connections* • TEC4110 • Key p. 63

MATTER: *Sink & float*   29

Name _____   Context clues, details, inferences

What do you know about magnets?

Words to Know
rectangle
opposite
metal

Mighty Magnets

How can you pick up a paper clip without touching it? With a magnet! A magnet pulls closer together things that are made of certain metals.

Magnets come in many shapes. Bar magnets look like rectangles. Horseshoe magnets look like the letter *U*. These kinds of magnets each have two ends. One end is called the north pole. One end is called the south pole. Some magnets are stronger than others. All magnets are strongest near the poles.

Sometimes magnets push things away. That is what happens when the north pole of one magnet is near the north pole of another. Only the opposite ends of magnets attract each other.

1. **Look** back in the passage. **Circle** the word that means "pull closer."

2. What are the two ends of a horseshoe magnet called? _____
   _____

3. **Read** each sentence below. **Circle** true or false.

   a. A magnet must touch an object to attract it.   true   false
   b. Magnets always pull things closer.   true   false
   c. The north pole of one magnet attracts the   true   false
      south pole of another.

   There are some things that magnets cannot pick up. Why? Write your answer on the back of this sheet.

Brain Builder

©2001 The Education Center, Inc. • *Comprehension Connections* • TEC4110 • Key p. 63

30 FORCES & ENERGY: *Magnets*

Name _____   Context clues, details, drawing conclusions

What are some ways that things can move?

Words to Know
spin   machine
direction

On the Move!

Wind can be a very strong force! A force is anything that pushes or pulls something else. People, animals, and machines can be forces, too.

Some forces move things in a straight line. A baseball player can throw a ball so that it goes right to first base. A dog can drop its ball so that it falls straight to the ground.

Other forces move things around and around. A child can spin a toy top. A merry-go-round goes in a circle.

Sometimes a force makes something change direction. A bike rider can turn the handlebars of his bike to make it go a different way.

Look closely and you will see forces all around you!

1. **Look** back in the passage. **Underline** the sentence that tells what a force is.
2. **Complete** each sentence with a word below. *(Hint: You will not use two of the words.)*

   | circle | move | direction | force | straight |

   a. A top moves in a _____.
   b. Forces can move things in a circle or in a _____ line.
   c. A mouse can be a _____.

3. **Think** about a leaf that falls from a tree. What might stop it from falling straight down? _____

Brain Builder

On the back of this sheet, draw a picture of something moving in a straight line and a picture of something moving in a circle. For each picture, write a sentence about the force.

©2001 The Education Center, Inc. • *Comprehension Connections* • TEC4110 • Key p. 63

FORCES & ENERGY: Kinds of motion 31

Name _____   Context clues, drawing conclusions, main idea

What makes things move more slowly or quickly?

Words to Know
forces   gravity
weight

Forces at Work

Some forces are stronger than others. Sometimes two forces try to move something at the same time. Think about a box. When a person tries to pick it up, the weight of the box pulls it down. The person needs to use a stronger force to lift the box.

Gravity is a strong force. It pulls most things toward Earth. When a person with a parachute jumps from an airplane, gravity pulls her down. She does not fall right to the ground like a rock, though. Air pushes up under the parachute at the same time that gravity pulls down. The air is not as strong as the gravity. That is why the jumper falls to the ground.

1. **Read** the words below. **Draw** a line from each word on the left to the matching group of words on the right.

   a. force •   • move something away
   b. push •   • force that pulls things toward the ground
   c. gravity •   • having a lot of power
   d. strong •   • anything that pushes or pulls something else

2. **Look** back in the passage. **Underline** the sentence that tells why the jumper falls even though air is pushing the parachute up.

3. If gravity were not as strong on Earth, what do you think would happen to someone who jumps from a plane with a parachute?
   _____
   _____

On the back of this sheet, use your own words to explain how a parachute helps someone jump from an airplane safely.

Brain Builder

©2001 The Education Center, Inc. • *Comprehension Connections* • TEC4110 • Key p. 63

32 **FORCES & ENERGY:** *Gravity*

Name _____   Classification, context clues, inferences

How did Native Americans live long ago?

Fishers, Farmers, and Hunters

Long ago there were no grocery stores. People got their food from the land and water. Many Native Americans in the Northeast lived near water. The tribes made canoes from tree bark. They used the boats to catch fish and lobsters.

Most of the land in the Southwest is dry. There are mountains and valleys. Some Native Americans farmed in the valleys. They grew a lot of corn.

The land in the western Plains is not good for growing crops. Buffalo was the main food for the Native Americans who lived there. The tribes hunted the buffalo on horses.

The land and water were important to every tribe. Each <u>region</u> gave the tribes something different!

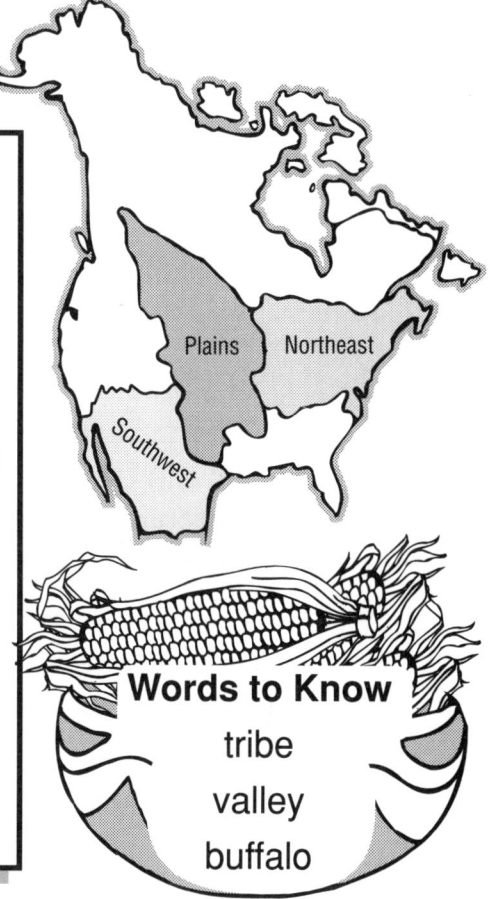

Words to Know
tribe
valley
buffalo

1. **Underline** the word in the passage that means "narrow boats."
2. **Look** at the underlined word in the passage. **Circle** the word below that means almost the same.

    food   place   store

3. **Think** about the passage. **Read** each word below. **Write** it in the best column.

corn	lobster	horse	buffalo	fish
dry	canoe	desert		hunt

Northeast	Southwest	Western Plains
_____	_____	_____
_____	_____	_____
_____	_____	_____

Brain Builder

Think about the passage. How was life in the Northeast different from life on the western Plains? Write your ideas on the back of this sheet.

©2001 The Education Center, Inc. • Comprehension Connections • TEC4110 • Key p. 63

CULTURE: *Native Americans*

Name _____ Details, following directions, main idea

How do people celebrate New Year's Day?

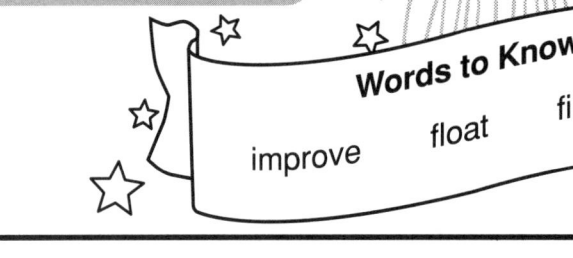

Words to Know: improve, float, fireworks

People all over the world love to celebrate holidays! Many people celebrate the New Year.

In the United States a lot of people promise to improve something in the New Year. A special parade is held on January 1. Each float in the parade is made with flowers!

The New Year lasts for 15 days in China. A lot of people decorate their homes with red for good luck. They have feasts. They set off fireworks, too.

Boys and girls in England sing to their neighbors on New Year's Day. The neighbors give them small gifts.

No matter where you live, the New Year is a time for a happy new start!

1. **Look** back in the passage. **Follow** the directions below.
   a. Use a red crayon to underline the place that has fireworks for New Year's Day.
   b. Use a blue crayon to underline the place that has a parade with a lot of flowers.
   c. Use a green crayon to underline the place where children sing on New Year's Day.

2. Why does the author call the New Year a time for a new start? _____
   _____

3. What is a good title for this passage? Why? _____
   _____

On the back of this sheet, draw and label three pictures to show how people celebrate the New Year in the United States, in China, and in England.

Brain Builder

©2001 The Education Center, Inc. • Comprehension Connections • TEC4110 • Key p. 63

34 CULTURE: *The New Year*

Name _____

What do you know about folktales?

Details, main idea

Stories From the Past

There were few books many years ago. There were a lot of stories, though! People shared the stories by telling them. These folktales were passed from person to person.

Sometimes people changed parts of a folktale when they told it. They changed the food, clothes, or names to be like the ones where they lived. They added things that were important in their countries.

The story of Cinderella is told in hundreds of ways. In some of the tales, a fairy godmother helps Cinderella. In a tale from China, a fish helps the girl. In a tale from Korea, an ox and a frog help her. Folktales can tell a lot about a place and the people who live there!

Words to Know
countries
Cinderella
ox

1. **Underline** the first sentence in the passage that tells how stories were passed from one person to another.

2. **Complete** each sentence with a word below. *(Hint: You will not use one of the words.)*

hundreds	countries	changed	folktale

   a. A _____ is a story that is passed from person to person.
   b. Sometimes one folktale is told in _____ of ways.
   c. People in many _____ share folktales.

3. Why do you think Cinderella is told in so many ways? _____

Brain Builder: How can you learn about a country from a folktale? Write your ideas on the back of this sheet.

CULTURE: *Folktales*

Name _____ Cause and effect, context clues, contrast

How are homes today different from homes in the past?

Words to Know
soil
settlers
prairie

Homes Past and Present

Do you know that 200 years ago some homes were made of grass and soil? American settlers made their homes from things in nature.

Some settlers lived on <u>prairies</u>. They cut blocks of grass and soil. They used mud to hold the <u>sod</u> blocks together. Other settlers lived where there were a lot of trees. They made log homes. Log homes were cleaner and stronger than sod homes. Some log homes had only one room. Later, people started to make houses with boards. Some of the homes had two <u>stories</u>.

Now there are many kinds of homes. Some people live in wooden or brick homes. Some people live in apartments or mobile homes. Some people even live on boats!

1. **Look** at the underlined words above. **Write** each one on the correct line.

    a. grass, roots, and dirt   _____

    b. floors of buildings   _____

    c. large grassy places   _____

2. Why were prairie homes different from forest homes? _____
   _____

3. What kinds of homes do people have today? **List** three of them from the passage.
   _____

On the back of this sheet, draw a picture of your home. Write two ways that it is different from homes in the past.

Brain Builder

Name _____ *Cause and effect, comparison and contrast*

What are some ways to travel on rivers?

River Travel

Long before there were cars and trains, a lot of pioneers moved west. They moved a long way to make new homes. It was hard for them to go through thick woods. Some pioneers used flatboats to go on rivers instead.

A whole family could ride on one flatboat. They used oars to move the boat. Sometimes when the family found a place to live, they took the boat apart. They used the wood to build a house on land.

Later, the steam engine was invented. People made boats with engines. Steamboats were faster than flatboats. They could carry many people and goods to the places they were going in less time.

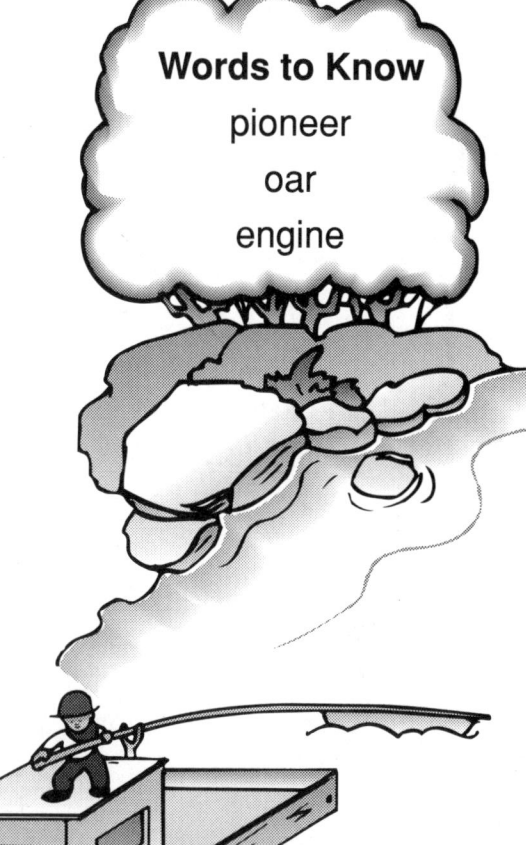

Words to Know
pioneer
oar
engine

1. **Look** back in the passage. **Underline** the sentence that tells why some pioneers traveled on the rivers and not through the woods.

2. How is a flatboat like a steamboat? _____
   _____

3. How is a flatboat different from a steamboat? _____
   _____

Brain Builder

How did the invention of the steam engine change things? Write your ideas on the back of this sheet.

Name _____ Details, drawing conclusions, main idea

How is bread made?

Words to Know
- grain
- dough
- bakery

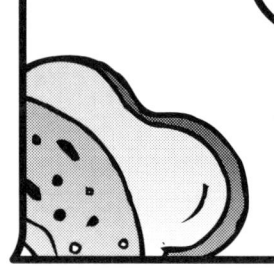

What food is more than 5,000 years old? Bread! People first made bread by mixing grain and water. They baked it on rocks in the sun. Years later, people started to bake bread in ovens. People called family bakers made bread. Each baker made dough. She took it to a bakery to be cooked. When the bread was done, she took it to people in her town.

Machines were later invented that could make bread quickly. Today, bakeries make many kinds of bread fast. Some of them have ovens that are bigger than buses! Machines move the bread through the ovens. When the bread is ready, trucks take it to stores.

1. Why was a family baker important to a town? _____
   _____

2. **Complete** each sentence with a word below. *(Hint: You will not use two of the words.)*

   | rocks | grain | bakeries | deliver | dough |

   a. Today trucks _____ bread to stores.

   b. Long ago bread was baked on _____.

   c. Now bread is made and cooked in _____.

3. What is a good title for this passage? Why? _____
   _____

Brain Builder
On the back of this sheet, draw a picture to show how bread was made long ago. Draw another picture that tells about bread today. Write a sentence for each picture.

Name _____

Details, drawing conclusions

How are cities different from the country?

Words to Know
urban rural
suburban

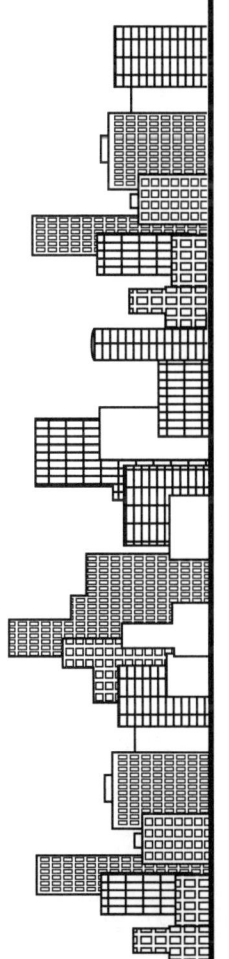

From Cities to Farms

What is it like where you live? Is it crowded? Is it quiet? The answers to these questions tell about your community. A community is a group of people who live in one place.

Some people live in cities. Cities are urban communities. They have a lot of people and tall buildings.

Some people live near cities. They live in suburban communities. Suburban communities are not as crowded as cities.

Other people live in rural communities. These places are in the country. Most people know each other. Some of them live on farms.

Big, medium, or small, everyone can find a community that is right for him!

1. **Look** back in the passage. **Underline** the sentence that tells what a community is.

2. **Look** back in the passage. **Circle** the word that means "close to."

3. **Draw** a line from each word on the left to the matching group of words.

   a. rural •   • many people and buildings
   b. urban •   • farms
   c. suburban •   • close to a city

4. **Think** about the passage. Why might a person want to live in a rural community?

Brain Builder

Think about the passage. What kind of community do you most want to live in: urban, suburban, or rural? Why? Write your answers on the back of this sheet.

GEOGRAPHY: *Rural, suburban, & urban communities*

Name _____ Details, inferences, main idea

How do you think the earth looked long ago?

Words to Know
change
pollution   soil

The Changing Earth

Earth does not look like it did many years ago! People change the earth in many ways. They make roads through mountains. They make beaches by lakes.

Sometimes people cut down trees to make new roads, stores, or homes. These changes give people more places to live and work. They give them more ways to travel.

The changes are harmful in some ways, though. New roads mean more cars and pollution. Some animals lose their homes when trees are cut down. Trees help keep soil in place. When a lot of trees are cut down, rain washes away the soil.

There is a lot to think about before we make more changes to the earth!

1. **Look** back in the passage. **Underline** the first sentence that tells why the earth does not look the same as it did long ago.

2. **Think** about the passage. What is one problem that happens if too many trees are cut down? _____

3. **Circle** the letter for the best ending to this sentence: The author wrote this passage to

   a. save the trees.
   b. show that a lot of changes have been made to our land.
   c. explain that changes to the earth are both helpful and harmful.
   d. help animals find new homes.

On the back of this sheet, draw a picture to show one way that people change the earth. Write if the change is helpful or harmful and why.

Brain Builder

GEOGRAPHY: *Man-made changes to the earth*

Name _____ Details, following directions, using a map

Why might you need to use a map?

Words to Know
symbol   direction
compass rose

Where, Oh Where?

Maps can help you find places all over the world! A map is a special drawing. Some maps look like pictures taken from the sky. Things appear much smaller on a map than they really are. It can be hard to fit a lot of places on a map. Symbols make it easier. Symbols are small pictures that stand for other things. A map key tells what each symbol means. A compass rose tells the direction of the places on the map. A map is a very useful tool!

Key
★ airport   ⌂ house
🌲 forest   ◯ lake
▦ railroad   ⬜s store

1. How can a map key help you? _____
   _____

2. **Look** back in the passage. **Underline** the sentence that tells how a compass rose is helpful.

3. **Look** at the map and key. **Answer** the questions below.
   a. **Start** at the lake. In what direction do you go to get to the forest?
   _____

   b. What street does the railroad cross?
   _____

   c. **Start** at the airport. In what direction do you go to get to the store?
   _____

Brain Builder

On the back of this sheet, explain what *symbol* means. Then turn your paper back over. Add a symbol to the map. List it in the key.

©2001 The Education Center, Inc. • *Comprehension Connections* • TEC4110 • Key p. 64

GEOGRAPHY: *Maps* 41

Name _____   Details, drawing conclusions

Where do people go to buy the things they need?

Words to Know
consumer
producer
service

TOYS

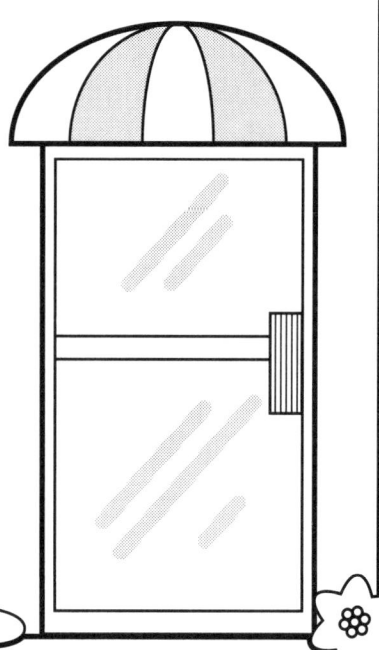

Shop Talk

People spend money in a lot of ways. Some people buy toys. Some people pay to have their lawns cut. Some people pay to see movies. People who buy things or pay for services are called consumers. If you use goods and services, you are a consumer.

You can see consumers in many places. You can see them in ice-cream shops, malls, and post offices. The people who work in these places help consumers get what they need. They are called producers. Producers provide goods or services. Doctors and booksellers are producers. Cooks and farmers are, too. There are consumers and producers in every town and city!

1. **Look** back in the passage. **Underline** the first sentence that tells what *consumers* means.

2. For each person below, **write** "producer" or "consumer."
    a. a man who pays to have his car washed _____
    b. a farmer who grows and sells corn _____
    c. a boy who sells lemonade _____
    d. a girl who buys a movie ticket _____

3. Why do producers need consumers? _____
   _____

Think about the producers you have seen. On the back of this sheet, draw and label pictures of three of them.

Brain Builder

ECONOMICS: *Producers & consumers*

Name _____

Context clues, details, sequencing

What steps are needed to get milk from farms to stores?

Words to Know
- spoil
- dairy
- cartons

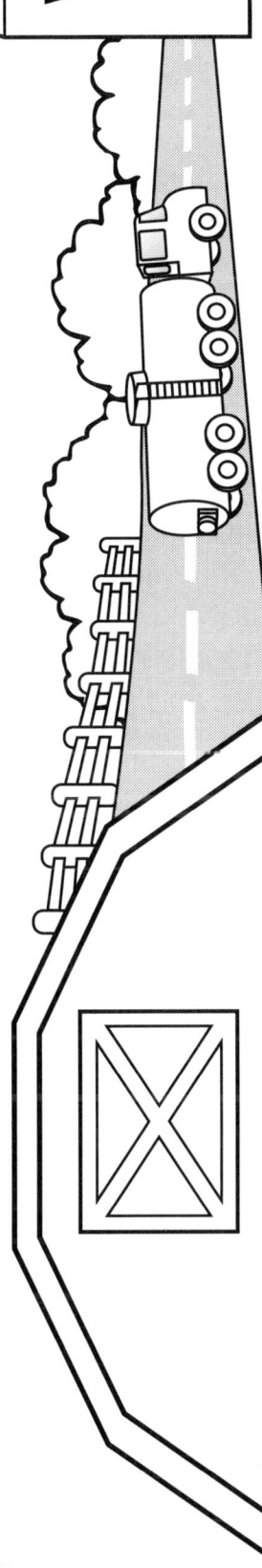

Please Pass the Milk!

You know that you can buy milk at a grocery store, but do you know how it gets there? Many steps need to be done to get milk from farms to stores. First, a farmer milks dairy cows. Most farmers use machines to do this. They put the milk in a cooling tank to keep it from spoiling. Next, a truck takes the milk to a dairy. Dairy workers use machines to clean the milk. Machines put it into cartons or plastic bottles. When it is ready, the milk is put on trucks and taken to stores. Workers unpack the milk and put it in coolers. Then consumers like you can buy it!

1. **Look** back in the passage. **Circle** the word that means "people who use goods or services."

2. What happens in a dairy?
   _____
   _____

3. **Number** the sentences below to show the correct order.
   a. ____ The milk is taken to a dairy.
   b. ____ The farmer uses a machine to milk the cows.
   c. ____ The milk goes into a cooling tank.
   d. ____ The milk goes on a truck to the store.
   e. ____ Machines clean the milk and put it into cartons.

Brain Builder

On the back of this sheet, draw pictures to show the steps needed to get milk from a farm to the houses in your neighborhood. Make the pictures look like a comic strip.

ECONOMICS: *Milk from cow to table*

©2001 The Education Center, Inc. • *Comprehension Connections* • TEC4110 • Key p. 64

Name _____   Context clues, main idea

What kinds of jobs are there?

Today's Special
Words to Know
train
needs
community

  Make believe that everyone works as a pizza maker. There would be a lot of pizza shops, but there would be no place to buy toys or clothes. No one would have the jobs to make or sell these things. There would be no doctors or teachers. No one would be trained to do these jobs.
  That is not the way it is, though! There are different jobs in every community. Some jobs are broken down into smaller jobs. Making pizza is a job like that. Some people produce the cheese, tomatoes, and other ingredients. Some people sell the ingredients. Other people mix and cook them. Big or small, every job helps meet people's wants and needs!

1. What is a good title for this passage? Why?

_____

_____

2. **Look** back in the passage. **Circle** the word that means "taught or shown how."

3. Why is it important for people in a community to have different jobs? **Circle** the letter for the best answer below.

   a. Some people are better at cooking than other people.
   b. Children need to go to school.
   c. Different jobs meet different needs and wants.
   d. Some people do not like pizza.

Think about the passage. On the back of this sheet, list four jobs that you think are important in a community. Write why you think so.

Brain Builder

©2001 The Education Center, Inc. • Comprehension Connections • TEC4110 • Key p. 64

44 **ECONOMICS:** *Division of labor*

Name _____   Comparison, context clues, drawing conclusions

What are some laws that you know?

Rules and Laws

Walk in the halls. Raise your hand. Use nice words. These are <u>rules</u> that some schools have. They help make sure that everyone is treated in a fair way. They help make sure that everyone stays <u>safe</u>. Rules for a city or a country do, too. These rules are called laws.

Many people <u>obey</u> laws every day. They may obey a lot of different laws just on the way to work! It is a law that cars must stop at red traffic lights and stop signs. There are laws about how fast cars can go. Laws help people know what they should do on the <u>roads</u> and many other places they go!

Words to Know
rule
obey
country

1. **Look** at the underlined words in the passage. **Write** each one on the correct line below.

   a. follow _____   c. streets _____

   b. not harmed _____   d. laws _____

2. **Underline** one of the school rules in the passage. **Write** why you think some schools have this rule.
   _____

3. **Write** two reasons that laws are important. _____
   _____
   _____

How are school rules and the laws for a country the same? Write your ideas on the back of this sheet.

©2001 The Education Center, Inc. • Comprehension Connections • TEC4110 • Key p. 64

CIVICS & GOVERNMENT: *Laws* 45

Name _____ Context clues, main idea

What are some things that good neighbors do?

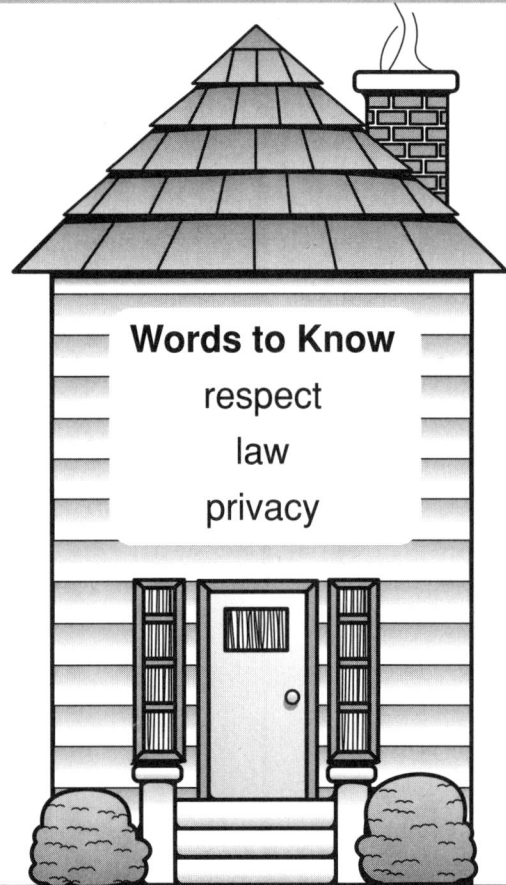

Words to Know
respect
law
privacy

Hello, Neighbor!

Think about the people who live near you. They are your neighbors. You and your neighbors are citizens of the same community.

Laws help keep citizens safe. They help keep communities clean. A good citizen obeys the laws. When he follows the laws, he helps make the community a nice place to be.

Good citizens show respect. A good citizen thinks about his neighbors' feelings. He respects their privacy. He respects the things that belong to them.

Good citizens also help each other. They work together to keep their neighborhood clean. They are careful not to make too much noise.

If you are a good citizen, people will like being your neighbor!

1. What does the word *neighbor* mean? _____
   _____

2. **Draw** an **X** in the box for each sentence below that tells about a good citizen.

   ☐ a. Hal leaves trash on the grass in the park.
   ☐ b. When Susan plays music, she keeps it soft.
   ☐ c. Jane helps Dan rake the leaves on his lawn.
   ☐ d. Sam used Ann's rake and did not return it.

3. **Think** about the passage. **Write** one way that a neighbor might show respect.
   _____

On the back of this sheet, draw two pictures that show how you can be a good neighbor. Write a sentence for each picture.

Brain Builder

©2001 The Education Center, Inc. • Comprehension Connections • TEC4110 • Key p. 64

CIVICS & GOVERNMENT: *Citizenship*

Name _____ *Context clues, main idea, drawing conclusions*

What do you know about the U.S. government?

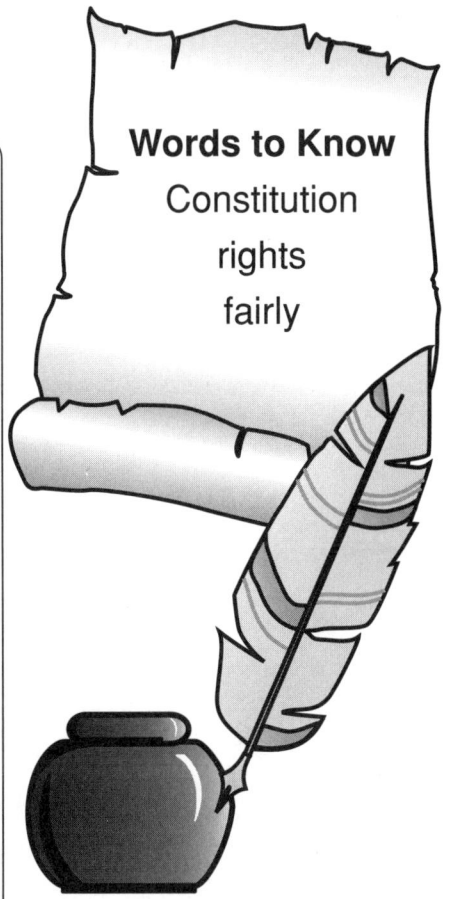

Words to Know
Constitution
rights
fairly

The U.S. Constitution

The main rules of the United States are written in the Constitution. It was written about 200 years ago. George Washington and several other men decided what it would say.

<u>The Constitution says that the U.S. government should have three branches</u>. The people who work in one part make laws. The people in the second part make sure the laws are followed. The people in the third part tell what the laws mean.

The Constitution gives people rights. A person has the right to go to the church he wants. He has the right to choose what he writes. He has the right to be treated fairly.

The Constitution is important to everyone in the United States!

1. **Look** at the underlined sentence in the passage. **Circle** the letter for the answer below that tells what *branches* means.

    a. trunks   b. goes a different way   c. parts

2. **Draw** a line from the beginning of each sentence to its ending.

    a. The Constitution tells •   • decide what would be in the Constitution.

    b. George Washington helped •   • to be treated in a fair way.

    c. People have the right •   • how the government should be run.

3. What is the Constitution mostly about? _____
   _____

Brain Builder

What do you think it would be like to live in the United States if there were no Constitution? Write your ideas on the back of this sheet.

©2001 The Education Center, Inc. • *Comprehension Connections* • TEC4110 • Key p. 64

CIVICS & GOVERNMENT: *U.S. Constitution*

Name _____   Comparison and contrast, details, inferences

What does "united" mean?

Words to Know
president
laws
governor

Fifty States United

The United States of America is a big country. It is made of 50 parts called states. The states are not the same size. Some states are large. Some states are small. All but two states touch at least one other state. The two states are Alaska and Hawaii.

All of the states are alike in some ways. Every state has cities, towns, and special places. Each state has its own lawmakers and governor. The governor is the leader of the state. The states have the same president. They all follow the laws of the United States. All 50 states work together to be one great country!

1. **Think** about the passage. **Answer** the questions.

    a. What is one way that all 50 states are alike? _____

    _____

    b. What is one way that the states are different? _____

    _____

2. **Look** back in the passage. **Underline** the sentence that tells about the job of a governor.

3. How many states touch at least one other state? _____

How did you decide on your answer for question number 3? Write your answer on the back of this sheet.

Brain Builder

©2001 The Education Center, Inc. • *Comprehension Connections* • TEC4110 • Key p. 64

48 THE UNITED STATES: *General information*

Name _____   Details, drawing conclusions, main idea

Why is the capital of a country important?

Words to Know
District of Columbia
Washington, DC
explorer

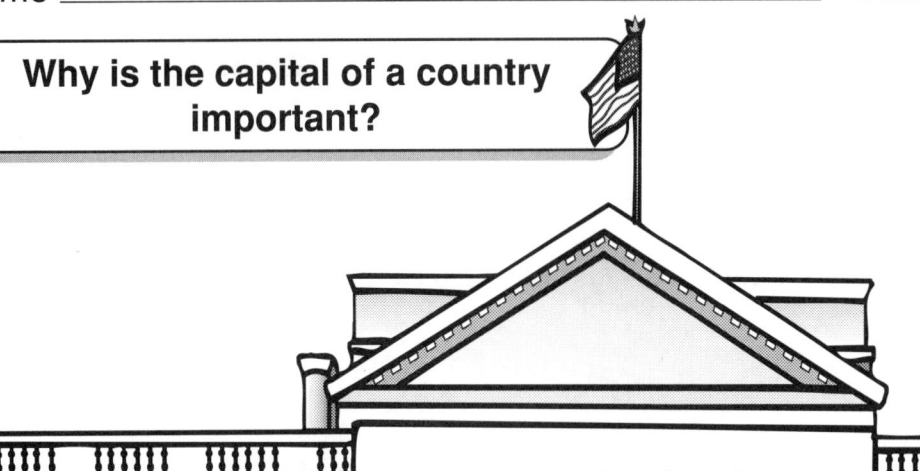

A Capital City

Washington, DC, is an important city. It is the capital of the United States. The city belongs to the whole country.

The city's name has two parts. The first part is named for George Washington. He was the first U.S. president. The second part has the letters *DC.* They stand for District of Columbia. This part is named for Christopher Columbus. He was an explorer.

Washington, DC, is a busy city. Laws are made there. It is where the U.S. president lives and works. There are a lot of museums. The museums teach people about history, art, and science. There is a lot to see and learn during a visit to the U.S. capital!

1. **Look** back in the passage. **Underline** the sentence that tells what the letters *DC* stand for in *Washington, DC.*

2. **Circle** the word in the passage that means "places where things that are important to history, science, or art are shown."

3. **Read** the words below. **Circle** three things you might see in Washington, DC.

   lawmakers   paintings   a lot of farmland   the U.S. president

4. Who was the U.S. capital named after? _____

_____

Brain Builder

How is Washington, DC, different from where you live? How is it the same? Write your thoughts on the back of this sheet.

©2001 The Education Center, Inc. • *Comprehension Connections* • TEC4110 • Key p. 64

THE UNITED STATES: *Capital* 49

Name _____   *Comparison and contrast, details, inference*

How is a sculpture of a person made?

Words to Know
carve   honor
Declaration of Independence

   Where can you see faces that are about as tall as five-story buildings? Mount Rushmore! Mount Rushmore is in South Dakota. It is a large stone sculpture. It took 14 years to carve. The workers used drills and dynamite to make it.
   Mount Rushmore honors four U.S. presidents. The first face on the left is George Washington. He was the first president. The next one is Thomas Jefferson. He was the third president. He wrote the Declaration of Independence. Teddy Roosevelt's sculpture is third. He was the 26th president. He helped end a war. The last sculpture is Abraham Lincoln. He was the 16th president. He helped end slavery. Mount Rushmore honors great men in a great big way!

1. **Underline** the words in the passage that tell how big Mount Rushmore is.

2. Why do you think the four faces were carved into Mount Rushmore?

   _____

3. **Read** the titles below. **Circle** the letter beside the best title for the passage.

   a. South Dakota   b. Men of Stone
   c. Fourteen Years   d. George Washington

4. **Read** the words below. **Circle** the letter for the words that best complete the sentence. The author wrote this passage to

   a. teach you about presidents.
   b. make you laugh.
   c. teach you about Mount Rushmore.

Make a poster for Mount Rushmore on the back of this sheet. Write on your poster three reasons why people should visit Mount Rushmore.

Brain Builder

©2001 The Education Center, Inc. • *Comprehension Connections* • TEC4110 • Key p. 64

THE UNITED STATES: *Mount Rushmore*

Name _____ Details, inferences, sequencing

Who was George Washington?

Words to Know
hero   surveyor
honor

The First U.S. President

What hero is shown on the quarter? George Washington is! George was born on February 22, 1732.

George had a lot of different jobs. First he was a farmer. Then he worked as a land surveyor. Next, George was a soldier. He was a soldier for five years. George later led the U.S. Army in a war. After the war, George became the first president of the United States. He was president for eight years.

People honor George in many ways. The U.S. capital is named for him. His picture is on the one-dollar bill. His birthday is celebrated on Presidents' Day. The "Father of Our Country" will always be remembered!

1. **Number** George Washington's jobs in the correct order.

    a. ____ soldier   c. ____ surveyor   e. ____ army leader
    b. ____ president   d. ____ farmer

2. **Circle** the word below that best tells about George.

    lazy   scared   brave   selfish   funny

3. **Look** at your answer for number 2. Why do you think this is the best answer?
    _____
    _____

4. **Look** back in the passage. **Underline** one way that people honor George.

Brain Builder

Think about the passage. Why do you think George is called the "Father of Our Country"? Write your ideas on the back of this sheet.

©2001 The Education Center, Inc. • Comprehension Connections • TEC4110 • Key p. 64

HISTORICAL FIGURES: *George Washington* 51

What do you know about Ben Franklin?

A Busy Man

Ben Franklin lived more than 200 years ago. Ben liked to read and think about new things. When he was eight years old, he started going to school. Ben went to school for two years. Then he worked in his father's shop making candles. Later, Ben worked in a print shop.

Ben wanted to make the United States a better place. He became a statesman. He helped write down the main laws of the United States. He also liked to experiment. Ben discovered that lightning is electricity. He invented a stove and a special pair of glasses.

Ben Franklin did a lot for his country!

Words to Know
experiment
statesman
electricity

1. **Draw** an **X** for each set of words below that tells about Ben. *(Hint: There are four of them.)*
   ____ a. wondered about new things   ____ b. invented things
   ____ c. was a fireman   ____ d. was president
   ____ e. worked as a statesman   ____ f. made candles

2. Why do you think Ben went to school for such a short time?
   _____

3. **Circle** the letter for the sentence that tells the main idea of this passage.
   a. Ben Franklin was a printer.
   b. Books were important to Ben.
   c. Ben Franklin helped the United States in many ways.
   d. Ben worked on a farm.

Ben Franklin was an inventor. What kind of person makes a good inventor? Why? Write your ideas on the back of this sheet.

Brain Builder

Name _____ Context clues, inferences, main idea

In what ways are your sight and hearing helpful to you?

Words to Know
deaf   Braille
raised

In the Dark

Make believe that it is dark and quiet. That is what life was like for Helen Keller. Helen got very sick when she was young. The illness made her blind and deaf. Helen was smart, but she could not talk.

When Helen was seven, a teacher helped her learn how to spell with her fingers. She taught Helen how to read and write Braille. Braille writing uses raised dots for letters and words. People read Braille with their fingers. Helen learned to speak when she was about 16.

Later, Helen went to college. She wrote books and gave talks about her life. She showed people that with hard work, many things are possible!

1. **Look** back in the passage. **Circle** the word that means "sickness."

2. Why do you think Helen could not talk when she was young? _____
   _____

3. Helen showed that people can do many things when they put their minds to it. What are two things that Helen was able to do because she worked hard?
   _____
   _____

On the back of this sheet, tell about Helen Keller in your own words. Draw a picture to go with your work.

©2001 The Education Center, Inc. • Comprehension Connections • TEC4110 • Key p. 64

HISTORICAL FIGURES: *Helen Keller* 53

Name _____   Comparison and contrast, details, drawing conclusions

What are some ways that radios are used?

Words to Know
wire   invent   tune

Tune In!

Long ago, the only way to quickly send a message far away was along a wire. There were many places that wires could not go. They could not go to ships at sea or to some places on land.

Then the radio was invented. It did not need wires. It helped people send messages over land and sea. News could reach a lot of people in a short time. People could tune in to hear shows and music, too.

When the TV was invented, some people thought that no one would use radios anymore. That was not so! Today people use them at home, at work, and in their cars. People use radios almost everywhere they go!

1. Why might it be important to send news quickly to a lot of people? **Circle** the letter for each correct answer below.

    a. A bad storm is on its way.
    b. People like to hear funny jokes.
    c. A main road is closed.

2. **List** two reasons that people use radios.

    _____
    _____

3. Why do you think some people thought that no one would use radios after the TV was invented?

    _____
    _____

How is a radio different from a TV? How is it the same? Write your ideas on the back of this sheet.

Brain Builder

54 **INVENTIONS:** *Radio*

Name _____ *Details, drawing conclusions, main idea*

How do you think books are printed?

Words to Know

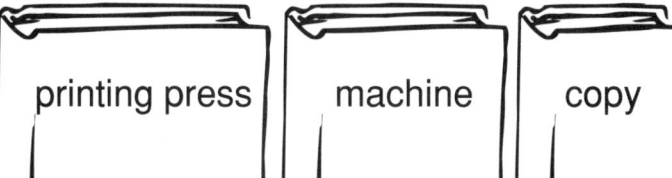
printing press | machine | copy

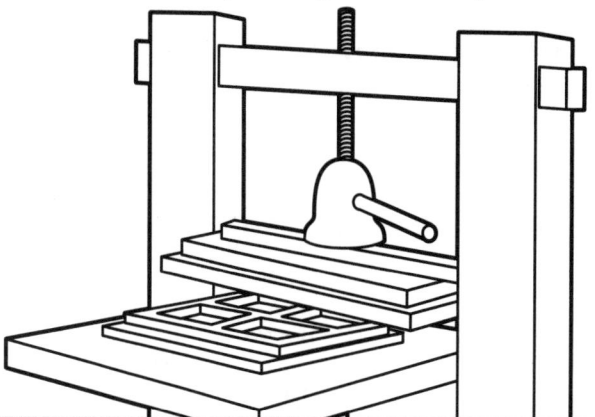

Make believe that you have to copy every word in a long book. Many years ago, that was the only way to make books. There were no machines to do the work. Writing a book by hand was hard. It took a long time. There were few books, and they cost a lot of money.

After the printing press was invented, it was easier to make books. Many copies could be made quickly. Books cost less. More people had books to read.

Today printing presses make copies of many things. Newspapers, road signs, cards, and T-shirts are all printed. You can see things that printing presses helped make everywhere you look!

1. There were not many books before the printing press was invented. **Circle** the letter for the sentence below that tells why.
   a. No one liked to read.
   b. The printing press made books quickly.
   c. Each book had to be written by hand.

2. Why did more people own books after the printing press was invented?
   _____
   _____

3. What is a good title for this passage? Why?
   _____
   _____

Brain Builder

Look around the classroom. What things do you think a printing press helped make? On the back of this sheet, list three of them. Draw pictures to go with your work.

©2001 The Education Center, Inc. • *Comprehension Connections* • TEC4110 • Key p. 64

INVENTIONS: *Printing press*

Name _____   Context clues, details, main idea

What do you know about sewing?

Words to Know
stitches
factory
even

Sew Easy!

Do you know someone who has a sewing machine? Many people have these handy machines. They use them to sew clothes and other things in a short time. Sewing has not always been quick, though. Long ago, the only way that people could sew was by hand. It took a long time. Then the sewing machine was invented. Some of the first machines could sew 200 stitches in one minute!

Today many factories use sewing machines. The machines make strong, even stitches. A lot of machines are used to make clothes. Some machines can sew boots, books, or rugs. At home or in a factory, the sewing machine is a great invention!

1. **Circle** the word in the passage that means "easy to use."

2. **Look** back in the passage. **Underline** the words that tell how people sewed before the sewing machine was invented.

3. Sewing machines can be used to make clothes. What else can they make? **List** three things named in the passage. _____
   _____

4. Why do you think the author titled the passage "Sew Easy!"? _____
   _____
   _____

Brain Builder

Do you think the sewing machine is an important invention? Why or why not? Write your ideas on the back of this sheet.

©2001 The Education Center, Inc. • Comprehension Connections • TEC4110 • Key p. 64

INVENTIONS: *Sewing machine*

Name _____   Details, drawing conclusions, summarizing

What does it mean to be brave?

Words to Know
pilot   flight   Atlantic Ocean

Hero in the Sky

Amelia Earhart was a brave woman. She liked to try new things. When she was young, flying was a new way to travel. Flying was not very safe. There were not many women pilots. That did not stop Amelia, though! She took flying lessons when she grew up. She worked hard to save money for a plane of her own. Amelia bought a bright yellow plane and called it the *Canary*. About ten years later, Amelia flew by herself across the Atlantic Ocean. Amelia was the first woman to make that flight alone.

1. **Look** back in the passage. **Underline** the first sentence that tells you Amelia lived a long time ago.

2. **Circle** the words in the passage that tell where Amelia flew alone.

3. Why do you think the author chose the title "Hero in the Sky"?
   _____
   _____

4. **Circle** the words below that tell about Amelia. *(Hint: There are three words.)*
   brave   lazy   police   scared   woman   pilot

On the back of this sheet, tell what you learned about Amelia Earhart in your own words.

©2001 The Education Center, Inc. • *Comprehension Connections* • TEC4110 • Key p. 64

FAMOUS FIRSTS: *Amelia Earhart* 57

Name _____

Context clues, details, main idea

What do you know about explorers?

_____

Words to Know
Arctic   North Pole   dream

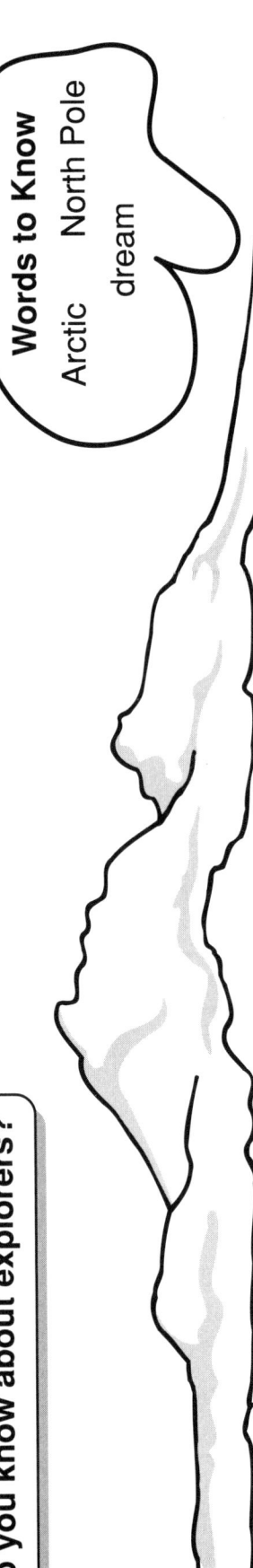

Top of the World

What is it like to go someplace that no one has ever been? Robert Peary and Matthew Henson knew. They were explorers.

Peary and Henson made a lot of trips to new places. One place they went was the Arctic. It is one of the coldest places on earth! They went there because they wanted to be the first people to stand at the North Pole.

The trip to the North Pole was long and hard. The ground was icy and dangerous. Sometimes it was only –62°F! Peary and Henson did not give up, though. On April 6, 1909, they reached the North Pole. Their dream came true!

1. **Look** at the underlined sentence in the passage. What does *hard* mean in this sentence? **Circle** the correct letter below to show your answer.
   a. solid   b. not easy   c. strict

2. Why was the trip to the North Pole dangerous? _____

3. **Read** the sentences below. **Circle** the letter beside the sentence that best tells the main idea of the passage.
   a. It is dangerous to go to the North Pole.
   b. Going new places is fun.
   c. Peary and Henson discovered the North Pole.

Brain Builder

Why do you think the author titled the passage "Top of the World"? Write your ideas on the back of this sheet.

©2001 The Education Center, Inc. • *Comprehension Connections* • TEC4110 • Key p. 64

FAMOUS FIRSTS: *Discovery of the North Pole*

Name _____   Context clues, drawing conclusions, sequencing

What does it mean to be an athlete?

Words to Know
gazelle   polio
paralyzed

A Winner

"She runs like a gazelle!" That is what many people said about Wilma Rudolph. She had not always been a fast runner, though. Wilma was sick a lot when she was young. Polio paralyzed one of her legs. Wilma's doctor did not think she would walk again.

Wilma wanted to run and play. She got a leg brace to help her walk. She exercised a lot. Finally, she could walk alone. Later, she could even run! When Wilma grew up, she won three gold medals at the Olympic® Games. She was the first American woman to do that. Who would have thought that a girl who could not walk would become a famous athlete!

1. **Look** back in the passage. **Circle** the word that means "known by a lot of people."

2. **Read** the words below. **Circle** the one that does <u>not</u> tell about Wilma Rudolph.
   winner   lazy   quick   athlete

3. **Read** the sentences below. **Number** them to show the correct order.
   ____ Wilma learned to run.   ____ She wore a leg brace.
   ____ Wilma won races.   ____ Wilma got polio.

4. Why do you think some people said Wilma was like a gazelle? _____
   _____

Pretend that you must tell a friend about Wilma Rudolph. What would you say? Write your ideas on the back of this sheet.

©2001 The Education Center, Inc. • *Comprehension Connections* • TEC4110 • Key p. 64

Name _____ *Graphic organizer*

At the Center!

Follow your teacher's directions to show what you read about.

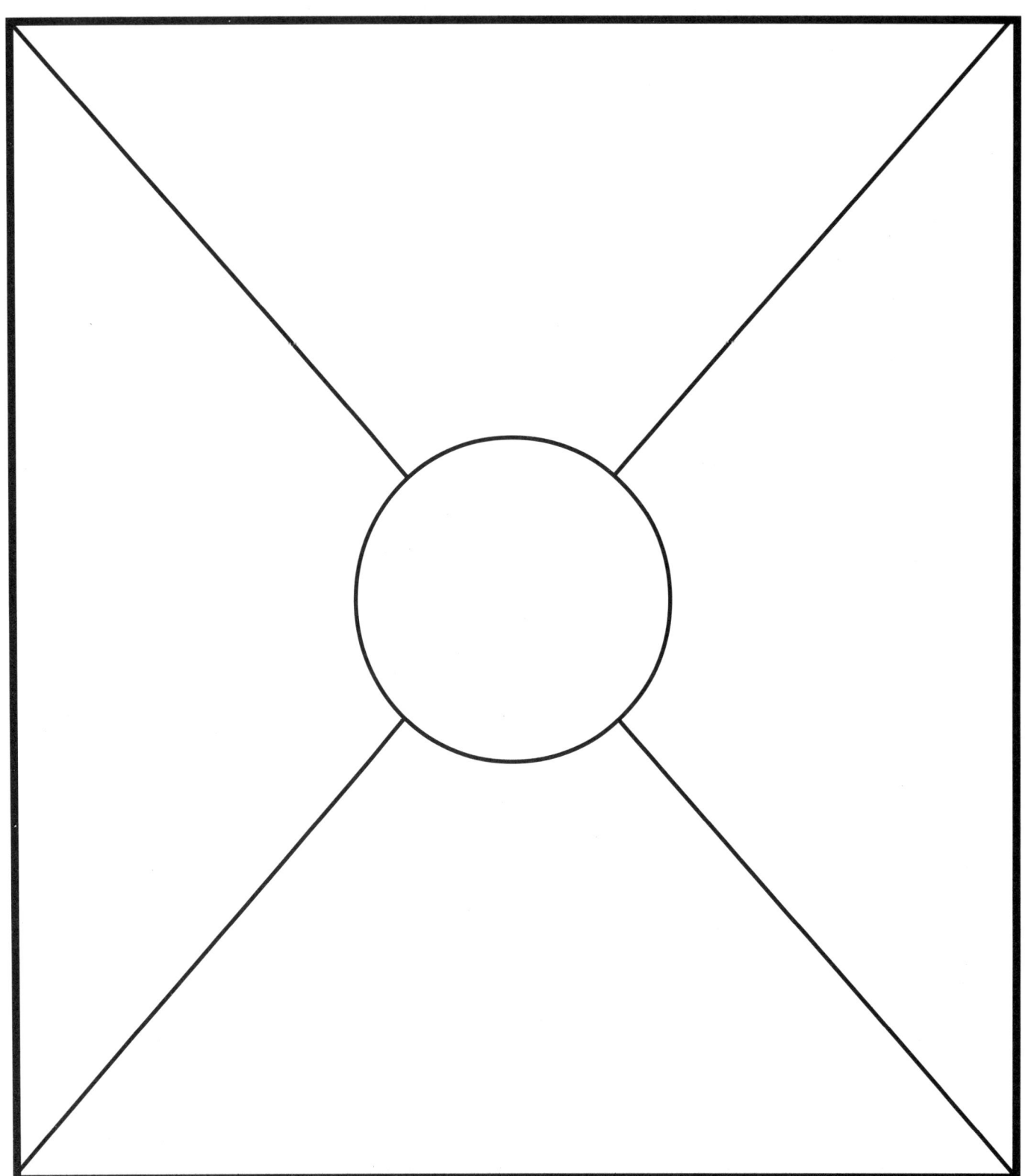

©2001 The Education Center, Inc. • *Comprehension Connections* • TEC4110

Note to the teacher: At the conclusion of a passage, give each student a copy of this sheet. The youngster writes the passage topic in the circle. In each remaining section, she writes a different word that relates to the topic and then uses it in a sentence. She adds an illustration for each one, if desired. Next, each youngster shares her work in a small group. Then a representative from each group tells the class about the similarities and differences among the group members' word choices.

Name _____

Graphic organizer

Get the Scoop on _____!

Follow your teacher's directions to tell about what you read.

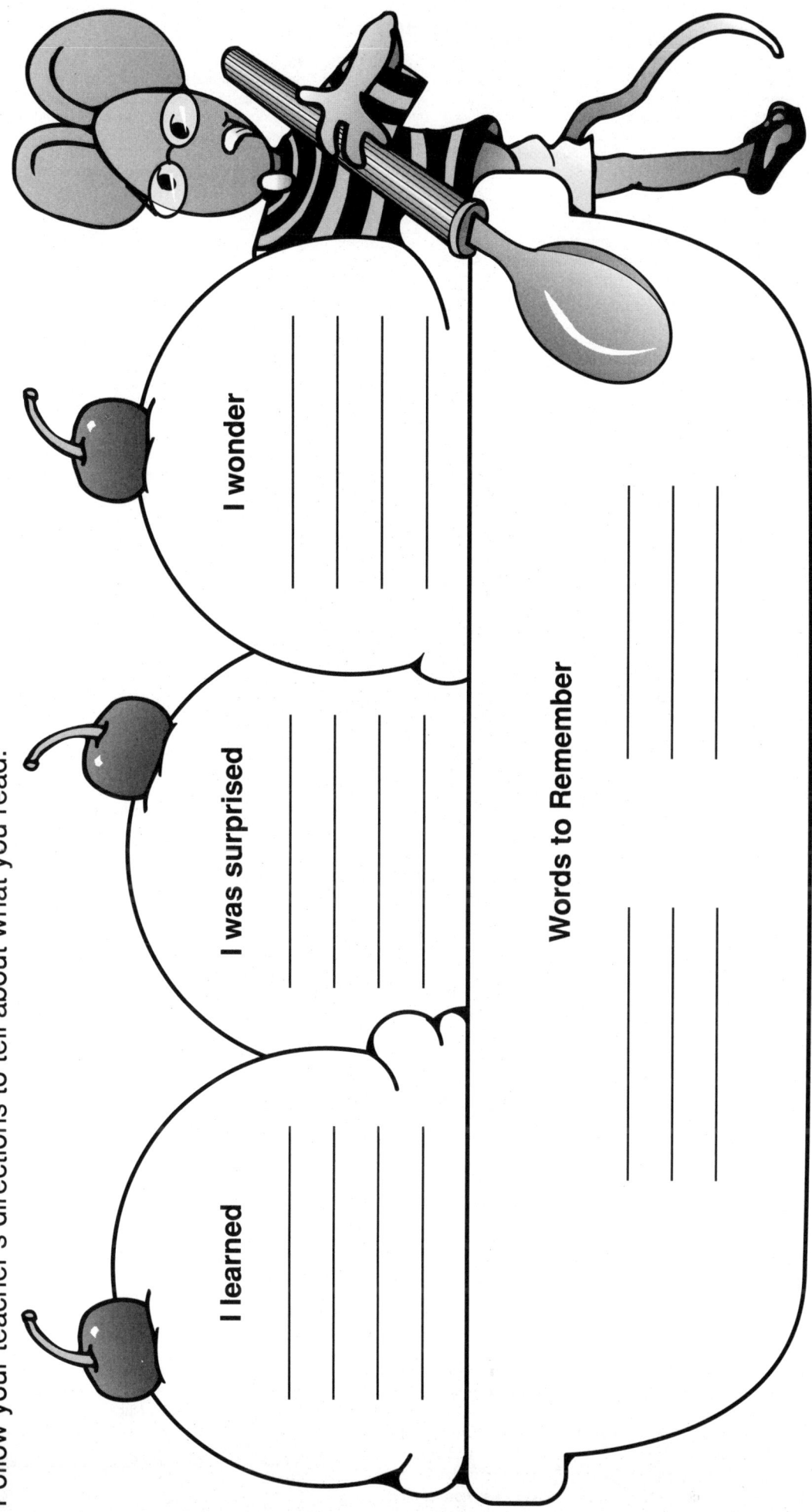

I learned

I was surprised

I wonder

Words to Remember

Note to the teacher: After students read an assigned passage or text, give each youngster a copy of this sheet. The youngster writes the reading topic on the provided line and completes the sentence on each ice-cream scoop. He lists key vocabulary terms or words that are new to him on the dish. Then pair students. Have each student share his sentences, read his words aloud, and explain to his partner his reasons for choosing the words.

©2001 The Education Center, Inc. • *Comprehension Connections* • TEC4110

Answer Keys

Page 6
1. c
2. air, water, food
3. People get food from plants and animals.
4. Answers will vary. Accept any reasonable responses.

Brain Builder: Drawings and sentences will vary but should reflect these basic needs: air, water, and food.

Page 7
1. through gills
2. frog
3. Answers will vary but should include that animals that live in water breathe through gills and animals that live on land breathe through lungs.

Brain Builder: Answers will vary. Accept any reasonable responses.

Page 8
1. habitat
2. a. country
   b. burrows
   c. safe
3. c

Brain Builder: Answers will vary. Accept any reasonable responses.

Page 9
1. a. holds up the flower
   b. helps feed the flower
   c. holds seeds
   d. makes new flowers
2. They hold a flower in the ground and take in water and food from the soil.
3. Answers will vary. Accept any reasonable responses.

Brain Builder: Answers will vary. Accept any reasonable responses.

Page 10
1. 3, 1, 4, 2
2. Spores look like tiny brown spots.
3. The life cycle of a rose begins with a seed, but the life cycle of a fern begins with a spore.

Brain Builder: Pictures should show a seed, a seedling, an adult plant, and a flowering plant.

Page 11
1. a. no
   b. yes
   c. no
   d. yes
   e. yes
2. They both hold seeds.

Brain Builder: Answers will vary. Answers may include the following: Pine trees have needles, but oak trees have leaves. The needles stay on the pine trees all year. The leaves change color and fall off the oak trees.

Page 12
1. change
2. a. survive
   b. Blubber
   c. thinner
3. b
4. Mammals need to adapt to their habitats to survive.

Brain Builder: Answers will vary. Accept any reasonable responses.

Page 13
1. Camouflage is a color, pattern, or shape. It helps a mammal blend into the environment.
2. protect
3. Mammals that are small, weak, or slow can use camouflage to protect themselves from enemies that are bigger, stronger, and faster.
4. Answers will vary. Accept any reasonable responses.

Brain Builder: Drawings will vary but should show that the hare is brown in the summer to blend in with the color of the dirt and rocks and white in the winter to blend in with the snow.

Page 14
1. observing
2. Accept any three of the following: Chimps hunt, use tools, solve problems, and have feelings.
3. Answers will vary. Accept any reasonable responses.
4. watchful, brave, scientist

Brain Builder: Answers will vary. Accept any reasonable responses.

Page 15
1. bees and butterflies
2. Insects carry pollen from plant to plant to make flowers and seeds.
3. Answers will vary. They may include that some insects eat parts of plants or that some insects lay their eggs on plants.
4. depend

Brain Builder: Answers will vary. Accept any reasonable responses.

Page 16
1. nymph
2. 4, 2, 1, 3
3. in water
4. An adult dragonfly can fly, but a nymph cannot.

Brain Builder: Drawings will vary but should depict the following sequence: a dragonfly nymph living in water, a dragonfly on a plant and shedding its skin, a dragonfly on a plant (waiting for its wings to strengthen), and a dragonfly flying away.

Page 17
1. crop
2. a. Some insects eat aphids.
   b. Some insects help plants make seeds.
3.

	friend	enemy
aphid		X
ladybug	X	
praying mantis	X	
bee	X	X

Brain Builder: Posters will vary. Accept any reasonable responses.

Page 18
1. extinct
2. a. asteroid
   b. reptiles
   c. Climate
3. a. fact
   b. opinion
   c. fact

Brain Builder: Answers will vary. Accept any reasonable responses.

Page 19
1. a. no
   b. no
   c. yes
   d. yes
2. Darwin's frog: swallows, hatches, tadpoles; Indian python: wraps, hatches, shakes

Brain Builder: Answers will vary. Accept any reasonable responses.

Page 20
1. metamorphosis
2. a. no
   b. no
   c. yes
3. Answers will vary. Accept any reasonable responses.

Brain Builder: Answers will vary. Accept any reasonable responses.

Page 21
1. a. weather vane
   b. thermometer
2. The passage is about weather forecasters and how they use tools to do their jobs.
3. c

Brain Builder: Answers will vary. Accept any reasonable responses.

Page 22
1. If cows lie down, it will rain.
2. hints
3. a. six more weeks of winter
   b. rain
   c. a nice day

Brain Builder: Answers will vary. Accept any reasonable responses.

Page 23
1. Answers will vary but should refer to cool clothing.
2. Thursday because clouds sometimes bring rain. Friday and Saturday because rainy and stormy weather is predicted.
3. wear a raincoat, fly a kite

Brain Builder: It got cooler during the week.

Page 24
1. a. constellations
   b. animals
2. hunter
3. The star pictures of his two dogs are near him.

Brain Builder: The stars are only part of the constellation because the imaginary lines are needed to complete the picture.

Page 25
1. Neptune, Jupiter, Mars, Saturn, Mercury, Venus, Uranus, Earth
2. a
3. Saturn is made of gas and is light for its size.
4. No spaceships have visited it. Pluto is far away and very small.

Brain Builder: Answers will vary. Accept any reasonable responses.

Page 26
1. point
2. c
3. orbit, rotate
4. Answers will vary. Accept any reasonable responses.

Brain Builder: Answers will vary. Accept any reasonable responses.

Page 27
1. a. false
   b. false
   c. true
   d. false
2. expand
3. liquid; It can be poured. It has the same shape as its container.

Brain Builder: a. Most gases are invisible.
b. Juice is the same shape as its container.
d. Some matter is heavy.

Page 28
1. a. change
   b. vapor
   c. Heat
2. a. liquid
   b. solid
   c. gas
3. You can change an ice cube into a liquid by exposing it to heat and causing it to melt.

Brain Builder: Ice cream melts as it gets warm, changing from a solid to a liquid.

Page 29
1. c
2. a clay boat
3. It would float because it would hold a lot of air.
4. The air inside a steel boat makes it less dense and able to float on water.

Brain Builder: Some things that are very big or heavy do not look like they will float, but they do.

Page 30
1. attract
2. They are called the north and south poles.
3. a. false
   b. false
   c. true

Brain Builder: The objects might not be made of a metal that is attracted to magnets, or the magnets might not be strong enough.

Page 31
1. A force is anything that pushes or pulls something else.
2. a. circle
   b. straight
   c. force
3. Wind might blow it in a different direction.

Brain Builder: Answers will vary. Accept any reasonable responses.

Page 32
1. a. anything that pushes or pulls something else
   b. move something away
   c. force that pulls things toward the ground
   d. having a lot of power
2. The air is not as strong as the gravity.
3. The person would fall more slowly.

Brain Builder: Answers will vary. Accept any reasonable responses.

Page 33
1. canoes
2. place
3. Northeast: lobster, fish, canoe; Southwest: corn, dry, desert; Western Plains: horse, buffalo, hunt

Brain Builder: Answers will vary. Accept any reasonable responses.

Page 34
1. a. China (red underline)
   b. United States (blue underline)
   c. England (green underline)
2. The holiday marks the beginning of a new year.
3. Answers will vary. Accept any reasonable responses.

Brain Builder: Drawings will vary. Accept any reasonable responses.

Page 35
1. People shared the stories by telling them.
2. a. folktale
   b. hundreds
   c. countries
3. Answers will vary. Accept any reasonable responses.

Brain Builder: The details in a folktale reflect the lifestyle and values of the people in a particular country.

Page 36
1. a. sod
   b. stories
   c. prairies
2. There were not many trees on the prairies, so the settlers could not make log homes.
3. Accept any three of the following: wooden homes, brick homes, apartments, mobile homes, or boat homes.

Brain Builder: Drawings and writing will vary. Accept any reasonable responses.

Page 37
1. It was hard for them to go through thick woods.
2. They are both forms of river transportation.
3. Answers will vary. Possible answers include the following: A flatboat moves by oars and a steamboat moves by an engine. A flatboat is slower than a steamboat.

Brain Builder: Answers will vary. Possible answers include the following: People could reach their destinations more quickly. More goods could be shipped in a shorter amount of time, which would increase business.

Page 38
1. A lot of people depended on her for their bread.
2. a. deliver
   b. rocks
   c. bakeries
3. Answers will vary. Accept any reasonable responses.

Brain Builder: Pictures and sentences will vary. Accept any reasonable responses.

Page 39
1. A community is a group of people who live in one place.
2. near
3. a. farms
   b. many people and buildings
   c. close to a city
4. Answers will vary. Accept any reasonable responses.

Brain Builder: Answers will vary. Accept any reasonable responses.

Page 40
1. People change the earth in many ways.
2. Answers will vary. Accept any of the following: The soil washes away. Animals lose their homes. More pollution is created.
3. c

Brain Builder: Pictures and writing will vary. Accept any reasonable responses.

Page 41
1. It tells what each symbol on a map means.
2. A compass rose tells the direction of the places on the map.
3. a. north
   b. Rocky Road
   c. east

Brain Builder: A symbol is a small picture that stands for something else. The student should have added a new symbol to the map and listed it in the key.

Page 42
1. People who buy things or pay for services are called consumers.
2. a. consumer
   b. producer
   c. producer
   d. consumer
3. They need consumers in order to make money.

Brain Builder: Pictures will vary. Accept any reasonable responses.

Page 43
1. consumers
2. Milk is cleaned and packaged in a dairy.
3. a. 3
   b. 1
   c. 2
   d. 5
   e. 4

Brain Builder: Pictures will vary. Accept any reasonable responses.

Page 44
1. Answers will vary. Accept any reasonable responses.
2. trained
3. c

Brain Builder: Answers will vary. Accept any reasonable responses.

Page 45
1. a. obey
   b. safe
   c. roads
   d. rules
2. Accept any one of the following sentences: Walk in the halls. Raise your hand. Use nice words.
3. Accept any two of the following: Laws help make sure that people are treated in a fair way. They help make sure that everyone stays safe. They help people know what they should do.

Brain Builder: Answers will vary. Accept any reasonable responses.

Page 46
1. A person who lives near someone else.
2. b, c
3. Answers will vary. Accept any reasonable responses.

Brain Builder: Pictures and writing will vary. Accept any reasonable responses.

Page 47
1. c
2. a. how the government should be run
   b. decide what would be in the Constitution
   c. to be treated in a fair way
3. The Constitution is about the main laws and government of the United States.

Brain Builder: Answers will vary. Accept any reasonable responses.

Page 48
1. a. Answers will vary. Possibilities include the following: Every state has cities, towns, and special places. Each state has a governor. Every state has the same president and follows the laws of the United States.
   b. Answers will vary. Possibilities include the following: The states are different sizes. Some states do not touch any other states. Each state has a different governor.
2. The governor is the leader of the state.
3. 48

Brain Builder: Answers will vary. Accept any reasonable responses.

Page 49
1. They stand for District of Columbia.
2. museums
3. lawmakers, paintings, the U.S. president
4. George Washington and Christopher Columbus

Brain Builder: Answers will vary. Accept any reasonable responses.

Page 50
1. about as tall as five-story buildings
2. Answers will vary. Accept any reasonable responses similar to the following: The faces were carved to honor four U.S. presidents who did great things.
3. b
4. c

Brain Builder: Posters will vary. Accept any reasonable responses.

Page 51
1. a. 3, b. 5, c. 2, d. 1, e. 4
2. brave
3. George needed to be brave when he was a soldier and when he led the army.
4. Accept any one of the following sentences: The U.S. capital is named for him. His picture is on the one-dollar bill. His birthday is celebrated on Presidents' Day.

Brain Builder: Answers will vary. Accept any reasonable responses.

Page 52
1. a, b, e, f
2. Possible answers include the following: His family could not afford to send him longer. His father needed Ben's help in the shop.
3. c

Brain Builder: Answers will vary. Accept any reasonable responses.

Page 53
1. illness
2. She could not hear so she had no model for speaking.
3. Accept any two of the following: Helen learned to read and write Braille, learned to speak, went to college, wrote books, gave talks, and helped others by her example.

Brain Builder: Pictures and writing will vary. Accept any reasonable responses.

Page 54
1. a, c
2. Answers will vary but may include the following: to listen to music, news, or shows.
3. Answers will vary. Accept any reasonable responses.

Brain Builder: Answers will vary. Accept any reasonable responses.

Page 55
1. c
2. There were more books and they cost less.
3. Answers will vary. Accept any reasonable responses.

Brain Builder: Answers will vary. Accept any reasonable responses.

Page 56
1. handy
2. by hand
3. boots, books, and rugs
4. Answers will vary. Accept any reasonable responses.

Brain Builder: Answers will vary. Accept any reasonable responses.

Page 57
1. When she was young, flying was a new way to travel.
2. across the Atlantic Ocean
3. Answers will vary. Accept any reasonable responses.
4. brave, woman, pilot

Brain Builder: Answers will vary. Accept any reasonable responses.

Page 58
1. b
2. Answers will vary but should include that it was very cold and icy.
3. c

Brain Builder: Possible answers include that the North Pole seems as though it is at the top of the world, or that Peary and Henson were so excited and proud that they felt as though they were "sitting on top of the world."

Page 59
1. famous
2. lazy
3. 3 Wilma learned to run.   2 She wore a leg brace.
   4 Wilma won races.   1 Wilma got polio.
4. A gazelle is an animal that runs very fast, and Wilma was a very fast runner.

Brain Builder: Answers will vary. Accept any reasonable responses.